1 & 2 THESSALONIANS

Discover Together Bible Study Series

Leader's guides are available at www.discovertogetherseries.com

DISCOVER TOGETHER

BIBLE STUDY

1 & 2 THESSALONIANS

Discovering Hope in a Promised Future

Sue Edwards

Poetry by Misty Hedrick

KREGEL
PUBLICATIONS

Library of Congress Cataloging-in-Publication Data
Names: Edwards, Sue, 1947- author.
Title: 1 and 2 Thessalonians : discovering hope in a promised future / Sue Edwards.
Description: Grand Rapids, MI : Kregel Publications, [2021] | Series: A discover together Bible studies | Includes bibliographical references.
Identifiers: LCCN 2020058592 | ISBN 9780825447112 (paperback)
Subjects: LCSH: Bible. Thessalonians--Study and teaching. | Hope--Biblical teaching.
Classification: LCC BS2725.55 .E39 2021 | DDC 227/.8106--dc23
LC record available at https://lccn.loc.gov/2020058592

ISBN 978-0-8254-4711-2

Printed in the United States of America
21 22 23 24 25 26 27 28 29 30 / 5 4 3 2 1

*"For I know the plans I have for you," declares
the* LORD, *"plans to prosper you and not to harm
you, plans to give you hope and a future."*
—Jeremiah 29:11

*Never has it been more important for God's people to
understand the prophetic word and to look for Christ's
appearing. People everywhere today have sobering, searching
questions about what the future holds. God's Word is the only
place we can find sure answers. Yet at the very time when
serious study . . . is most needed, its importance has diminished
in many churches and in the lives of many Christians.*
—Mark Hitchcock, The End

Contents

Why and How
to Study the Bible

Varied voices perpetually shout for our attention. Whose voice deserves our trust? The politician or evangelist on television? The Wall Street CEO? The Uber driver we've never met but count on to take us home? The man hawking cell phones behind the counter? The woman on the treadmill beside us? Maybe we can trust them; maybe we can't. Over time we can discern whether or not we're comfortable inviting them into our personal space or giving weight to their opinions. But the reality is that in time, everyone will disappoint us, and we will disappoint them too.

Only one is perfectly trustworthy. Only one offers authentic hope. "Therefore, with minds that are alert and fully sober, set your hope on the grace to be brought to you when Jesus Christ is revealed at his coming" (1 Peter 1:13).

Years ago, a wise woman, who secretly paid for my daughters to attend a Christian school we couldn't afford, planted that truth in my mind and heart. This concept blossomed into realistic expectations for life and a hearty hunger for a relationship with that one trustworthy person. That hunger led to a lifetime of savoring God's Love Letter, the Scriptures, and that relationship and practice upended everything. Wherever you are in your journey, Jesus invites you to experience abundant life with him. How?

Come with me to Thessalonica to discover hope in your promised future.

How to Get the Most Out of a Discover Together Bible Study

We're all at different junctures in our spiritual journeys, but God's Word doesn't separate us according to superficial differences. We all want to know God intimately and flourish, and we can all learn from one another. "As iron sharpens iron, so one person sharpens another" (Proverbs 27:17).

Discover Together Bible studies are designed to promote unity, for all women to learn from and enjoy together regardless of age, stage, race, nationality, spiritual maturity, or economic or educational status. God proclaims we are all sisters in his forever family, preparing to spend eternity together (Matthew 12:46–50).

However, our schedules vary week to week depending on the needs of loved ones, travel responsibilities, and work demands. To honor these differences, this study provides two choices:

- Basic questions that require between one to one and a half hours of prep a week, offering in-depth Bible study with a minimum time commitment
- "Digging Deeper" questions for women who want to probe the text more deeply

Women wanting to tackle the "Digging Deeper" questions may

- need resources such as an atlas, Bible dictionary, or concordance;
- check online resources and compare parallel passages for additional insight;
- use an interlinear Greek-English text or *Vine's Expository Dictionary* to do word studies;
- grapple with complex theological issues and differing views; and
- create outlines and charts and write essays worthy of seminarians.

In addition to God's Love Letter, we also need authentic community and a place to be ourselves, where we are loved unconditionally despite our differences and challenged to grow.

This Bible study is designed for both individual and group discovery, but you will benefit more if you complete each week's lesson on your own and then meet with other women to share insights, struggles, and aha moments.

If you choose to meet together, someone needs to lead the group. You will find a free downloadable leader's guide for each study, along with tips for facilitating small groups with excellence, at www.discovertogether series.com.

Choose a realistic level of Bible study that fits your schedule. You may want to finish the basic questions first and then dig deeper as time permits. Take time to savor the questions, and don't rush through the application.

Read the sidebars for additional insight to enrich the experience. Note the optional passages to memorize, and determine if this discipline would be helpful for you.

Do not allow yourself to be intimidated by women who have walked with the Lord longer, who have more time, or who are gifted differently. You bring something to the table no one else can contribute.

Make your study top priority. Consider spacing your study throughout the week to allow time to ponder and meditate on what the Holy Spirit is teaching you. Do not make other appointments during the group Bible study. Ask God to enable you to attend faithfully.

Come with an excitement to learn from others and a desire to share yourself and your journey. Give it your best to find the only one who will never let you down.

WHAT IS INDUCTIVE STUDY, AND WHY IS IT SO POWERFUL?

The Discover Together series uses inductive Bible study as a structure to dig into the Bible. Inductive study is the practice of investigating or interviewing a Bible passage to determine its true meaning, attempting to leave behind any presuppositions or personal agendas.

First, we seek to learn what the original author meant when writing to the original audience. We carefully examine the words and ideas. We ask questions like, What is happening? Who is it happening to? And where is it happening? Only after we answer those questions are we ready to discern what we think God meant.

And once we are clear about what God meant, then we are ready to apply these truths to our present circumstances, trusting that a steady diet of truth will result in an enriched relationship with Almighty God and beneficial changes in our character, actions, and attitudes.

Inductive study is powerful because discerning biblical truth is the best way we grow in faith, thrive in our lives, and deepen our relationship with the God who created us.

To experience this powerful process, we must immerse ourselves in the practice of study as a lifestyle—and not just focus on a verse here and there. Our life goal must be to digest the Bible, whole book by whole book, as life-giving nourishment that cannot be attained any other way.

Over a span of sixteen hundred years, God orchestrated the creation of sixty-six biblical documents written by the Holy Spirit through more than forty human authors who came from different backgrounds. Together they produced a unified Love Letter that communicates without error God's affection, grace, direction, truth, and wisdom. He did this so that we would not be left without access to his mind and heart (Hendricks and Hendricks, *Living by the Book*, 23).

THE INCREDIBLE BENEFITS OF BIBLICAL LITERACY

Earning a quality education changes us. It makes us literate and alters our future. Many of us sacrifice years, money, and energy to educate ourselves because we understand education's benefits and rewards.

Biblical literacy is even more valuable than secular education! But just like with secular learning, becoming biblically literate requires serious investment. However, the life-changing rewards and benefits far outweigh a diploma and increased lifetime earnings from the most prestigious Ivy League university.

A few benefits to Bible study include

- a more intimate relationship with Almighty God;
- an understanding of the way the world works and how to live well in it;
- a supernatural ability to love ourselves and others;
- insight into our own sin nature along with a path to overcome it, and when we fail, a way to wipe the shame slate clean, pick ourselves up forgiven, and move on with renewed hope;
- meaning and purpose;
- relational health experienced in community;
- support through struggles;
- continued growth in becoming a person who exhibits the fruit of the Spirit: love, joy, peace, patience, kindness, goodness, faithfulness, gentleness, and self-control (Galatians 5:22–23); and
- contentment as we learn to trust in God's providential care.

Every book of the Bible provides another layer in the scaffolding of truth that transforms our minds, hearts, attitudes, and actions. What truths wait to be unearthed in these two letters to the Thessalonians, and how will they change us?

Why Study
1 and 2 Thessalonians?

We don't have to live life too long before we learn that we can't count on things we thought we could count on. In just a few days, everything can change. In just a few days, we can lose hope.

What do you count on?

Your job—it might not be here tomorrow.
Your health—some unexpected disease might claim you overnight.
Your family—you might not be able to see them.
Your friends—they might get sick too.
Your savings—it might be gone in a stock market crash.
Your amusements—they might be closed.
Your traditions—they might be canceled.
Your staples—they might not be available.
Your luxuries—they might be on back order.

Which of life's difficult experiences have you endured? What did you learn about yourself during those times?

Some people implode. Suicides soar. Abuse and domestic violence hide behind closed doors. Liquor store shelves are pillaged and curbsides pile high with beer, wine, and hard liquor cartons. And emotions run high: sadness, depression, disappointment, hopelessness.

When you're struggling, do any of these emotions sneak up and kidnap you? Probably most of us battle some anxiety, a normal response to crisis. Because of my early history of depression, I always wonder how I'll cope when life goes dark or when an unexpected trial pops up or when I'm ambushed by a struggle. I usually feel sad off and on, but thankfully I've learned to immerse myself in prayer, study, productive projects, and service. They keep me from falling into a pit of hopelessness. How about you?

We never know what challenges lie around the corner. Would you like to arm yourself for tomorrow? Would you like to trust that God will

I feel right at home in Thessalonica because I lived in Greece in my middle school and early high school years. My father was stationed on the Coast Guard cutter USS *Courier*, a Voice of America ship that broadcast behind the Iron Curtain during the Cold War. We lived on the Aegean island of Rhodes, where I spent afternoons snorkeling in the blue-green ocean, biking with friends around the island, exploring ancient ruins, and interacting with the Greek people, who came to love and protect us as the children of the Americans. I didn't know that I was walking in the steps of Paul, who visited Rhodes on one of his mission trips. Now that I'm a believer, I treasure those experiences—they bring alive the places Paul visited, and they enrich my study of Scripture. I hope my experiences in Greece will benefit you, too, as I lead you through our Thessalonian adventure. —Sue

provide a lifeline of hope however deep the pit? If you'd like to find hope in a promised future, come with me to Thessalonica.

> Brothers and sisters, we do not want you to be uninformed . . . so that you do not grieve like the rest of mankind, who have no hope. (1 Thessalonians 4:13)

PREPARE FOR THE JOURNEY

Join me as we stroll arm in arm along the boulevard in Thessalonica, the second-largest city in Greece today. On our left, playful waves introduce gemlike turquoise waters to white-pebbled beaches. On our right, we stop for a leisurely Greek coffee or lemonada at an outdoor café or enjoy an English-language film at one of their cinemas. After all, Thessaloniki hosts its renowned film festival October through November.

What would make our trip more meaningful than an exciting holiday? The realization that we are walking in the footsteps of Paul.

We arrived by air or cruise ship, but Paul entered on foot almost two thousand years ago with two weary sidekicks, Silas and Timothy, after a grueling five-day walk from Philippi. Paul had just begun his second missionary trip, and he never intended to step foot into this part of Greece, called Macedonia. He probably planned to plant new churches or revisit churches he'd birthed during his first missionary trip throughout eastern regions of what is now Turkey. But just as God has his unique way of guiding each of us, God led Paul west by orchestrating a vision of a man pleading with Paul: "Come over to Macedonia and help us" (Acts 16:9). Moved by this dream, Paul and his mentees packed up the next day and crossed the border into Europe. God's plan was bigger than Paul's.

During their initial days in Thessalonica, Paul likely wandered through the city looking for clues to better understand the people he hoped to reach with the gospel. Polytheism was common for most Greeks, and their idols adorned every corner. Mount Olympus, the highest mountain in Greece, was believed to be the place Zeus regularly gathered his pantheon of gods. On a clear day, Paul could face southeast and view the summit of Olympus.

If Paul and his companions eavesdropped on conversations, they might have heard townsfolk speculating about ways to placate the anger and win the favor of their fickle gods. Soon Paul would show them the beautiful character of the one true God and that cyclonic gospel message would sweep through the city. Some would believe, their lives upended for eternity. Others would be so threatened, they would form murderous coalitions to silence these intruders.

As full of intrigue and drama as any Netflix series, these two letters reveal how God used early Christians to plant the seeds that four hundred years later would uproot the ferocious Roman Empire and ultimately spread the gospel throughout the world.

Google Thessalonica (thessaloniki.travel) to see photographs of this modern-day city and tourist sites you might one day enjoy visiting.

One of Alexander the Great's army officers founded the city in the fourth century BC. He named it after his wife, Thessalonica, who was Alexander's half sister. Similar to the Old Testament books of Esther and Ruth, these two letters to the Thessalonians are named after a famous woman. Most scholars believe Paul and his companions arrived around AD 50. He often chose influential cities, like Thessalonica, to plant churches. The city of two hundred thousand was the capital of Macedonia and a flourishing commercial center with a bustling seaport. It was situated on a major stone highway connecting Rome to the East, the *Via Egnatia*, or Egnatian Way. Should a Christian church thrive there, chances were that smaller churches would spring up throughout the surrounding area.

DIFFERENT PERSPECTIVES ABOUT THE END TIMES

With the exception of the book of Revelation, Paul's letters to the Thessalonians reveal more details about your future than any other book in the Bible. Understanding these beautiful future realities gives us hope to persevere in difficult times and something to look forward to.

But respected scholars and pastors hold different views about how to interpret the Bible regarding the end times. Should we interpret these particular passages literally or figuratively? When will these events occur—in the future, or have they already occurred? How do all the pieces fit together?

Below are some of the varied interpretations.

Four views on when or if end times events will occur:
1. These events will really happen in the future.
    - This approach consistently interprets the Bible literally, attempting to understand first what the original author was communicating to the original audience and then what that text means for us today.
    - If the original author seemed to be using figurative language, then interpreters take that into account, but otherwise interpreters believe the passage means what it says.
    - Known as the futurist view.
2. These events won't ever really happen; they only teach spiritual principles.
    - The Thessalonian letters teach timeless spiritual lessons and principles that help Christians understand great historical themes and the ultimate triumph of good over evil.
    - These principles help believers live well today in a world full of challenges and struggles.
    - Known as the idealist or spiritualist view.
3. These events already happened.
    - These prophecies were fulfilled by ancient catastrophic events, like the destruction of Jerusalem in AD 70.
    - Known as the preterist view.

4. These events are happening now.
   - These prophecies are being fulfilled by the atrocities, barbarism, chaos, and turmoil we are experiencing now during the church age.
   - Known as the historicist view.

Three views on the idea of a real millennial kingdom:

Revelation 20:1–6 talks about Christ ruling a thousand-year kingdom on the earth. Is this a real kingdom that will actually last one thousand years? Will this occur in the future, is it already here, or is it in process?

1. A literal thousand-year kingdom will occur in the future.
   - After Christians are raptured, they will spend seven years with God in heaven while those on earth will endure a seven-year period of great suffering and destruction known as the great tribulation described in the book of Revelation. Then Christians will return to earth with Christ from the heavenly realms to establish and reign over a thousand-year kingdom on the earth, a time of unprecedented peace and justice.
   - Known as the premillennial view.
2. The kingdom is in process now.
   - The present earth is becoming better and better as Christians spread the gospel around the world. In time we will usher in a golden age of peace and prosperity. Then Christ will return to take believers into eternal bliss.
   - Known as the postmillennial view.
3. The kingdom reigns in our hearts now.
   - The kingdom that Paul and other biblical authors mentioned is spiritual in nature. It already exists since Christ came to earth to reign in Christians' hearts.
   - When we die, we go to a place of eternal bliss, called heaven.
   - Known as the amillennial view.

Three views on when the rapture will occur:

Paul taught the Thessalonians about an event theologians call "the rapture," which means "snatching away" (1 Thessalonians 4:13–5:11). If we interpret what Paul and others write literally, we can conclude:

- This event will occur suddenly when Christ calls all believers to leave the earth when he takes them away to a place we call heaven.
- There we wait with him for the time when he will bring us back to earth to set up his millennial kingdom.
- During the wait, believers in their glorified, resurrected bodies will experience perfect communion with God and other

believers, as well as spectacular events described in the book of Revelation.

Theologians who believe in a literal thousand-year millennial kingdom debate whether the rapture will occur before, during, or after the seven-year tribulation. The three main views are these:

1. The rapture will occur before the tribulation (pretribulation view).

2. The rapture will occur in the middle of the tribulation (mid-tribulation view).

3. The rapture will occur at the end of the tribulation (posttribulation view).

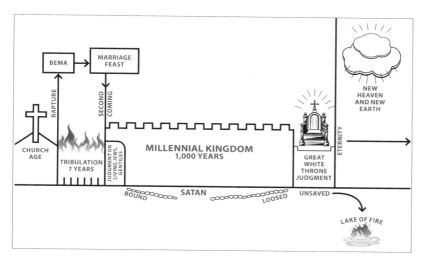

THE AUTHOR'S PERSPECTIVE

Some Christian doctrines are central to the faith—for example, the virgin birth, Christ's atonement, and the return of Christ, but others are disputable. That means that respected, godly scholars who believe in the inerrancy of the Bible disagree on some of the details. Christians tend not to break fellowship with other believers on these disputable matters.

That said, prophecies about what will happen in the future are all through the Bible, and I find them indescribably comforting and life-giving as I navigate the complex maze of living in a fallen world. When I'm discouraged and need hope, looking ahead to the glorious future my Jesus has planned for me enables me to look up and push forward.

I hold a premillennial, pretribulation view. That means I believe the end times events will occur in the future. That includes a literal one-thousand-year kingdom on the earth led by King Jesus, a place of yearned-for justice and peace. He establishes this kingdom after the tribulation, a time of horrendous chaos and judgment. However, out of his divine love and mercy, Jesus takes the church from the earth first, and believers will return with him to set up the kingdom.

HOW TO DISAGREE AGREEABLY

If you work through this study with others, they may express different opinions. Allow them the freedom to articulate their ideas. Listen with respect to everyone. Create a safe place where honest dialogue thrives. Trust the Holy Spirit to teach each of you as you gather to learn and encourage one another. Don't be afraid to gently disagree, but focus on the ideas and don't allow these differences to elevate into personal disputes. Love one another and refuse to sacrifice your unity over disputable matters. At the same time, speak up kindly concerning what you believe and why. As we say in our seminary, "Teach truth; love well."

1 THESSALONIANS

Hope Comes to Thessalonica

Hope is the thing with feathers
That perches in the soul,
and sings the tune without the words,
and never stops at all.
—Emily Dickinson (1830–1886)

OPTIONAL

Memorize Romans 15:13
May the God of hope fill you with all joy and peace as you trust in him, so that you may overflow with hope by the power of the Holy Spirit.

Hope is like oxygen. It enables us to survive and even thrive in a fallen world. Paul brought that hope to our brothers and sisters in first-century Thessalonica, and Jesus offers us that same hope today.

Imagine you travel from city to city in a distant country because you have discovered a truth that's revolutionized your life and you want to share it with others. You march into each city, find a place of worship, and convince the leaders there to let you make your case for these marvelous truths you want them to understand. As you can imagine, your reception varies. Some love you. Others, not so much, especially when your message contradicts the teaching of the established leaders. Factions form. Over and over you enrage so many people that they throw you out of town.

Paul has just experienced this scenario—again. His home base, First Church of Antioch, has commissioned him for a second missionary trip. He's on his way east when God unexpectedly calls him to go west into Europe. First stop, Philippi: Riots, flogging, placed in stocks and jail, a miraculous escape, and voila—First Church of Philippi is born. Then the authorities chased Paul out of town.

As a result, Paul and his companions head south to the next large city, Thessalonica—a five-day journey along the Roman road called the Egnatian Way. But before we delve into Paul's letters, let's discover how this church began.

 Read Acts 17:1–14.

1. Where did Paul and his companions go on the first Sabbath when they arrived in Thessalonica? What were the big ideas of his sermons? What does this reveal about Paul (17:1–3)?

2. Who attended his three-Sabbath sermon series, and how did the different groups respond (17:4–5)? What are the benefits of different kinds of people coming together to form a church? What are the challenges?

3. What actions did the adversarial group take (17:5)? What do you learn about the hostile Jews' ethics from their charges (17:6–9)? If you made a movie of this drama, who would you ask to play the various parts?

4. Any ideas why the author only mentioned Jason's first name in verses 5–6? What can you surmise about him from this account (his financial status, his spiritual maturity, etc.)?

5. Under cover of darkness, the Thessalonian believers hustled Paul and Silas off to Berea, another fair-sized city in Macedonia. What pattern do you see repeated there (17:10–14)?

6. What have you learned about Paul and his adversaries from your study so far? List these character qualities on the chart below.

Paul	Paul's Adversaries

7. How are you like and/or unlike Paul? His rivals? Which of these qualities would you like to develop and emulate? Which do you need to extinguish or avoid?

8. From this account, what can you learn about the following:

How to share your faith?

How to handle conflict?

The same group who attacked Paul in Thessalonica followed him to Berea and caused him trouble there too. After being thrown out of Berea, Paul escaped to Athens. He then traveled to Corinth, where he planted another church and remained for several years. But he never forgot his dear brothers and sisters in Thessalonica.

Had the seeds he'd planted in the short time he was there sprouted? Were they able to weather the same powerful opposition he had experienced? Had his teaching taken root? Were they living out what they had learned? Too risky to go back himself, Paul sent Timothy to find out—and praise God, Timothy brought back exciting news.

In response, Paul wrote letters to the Thessalonian Christians—the first within a year of when he left. We find answers to Paul's questions in those letters.

 **Read 1 Thessalonians 1.**

9. Although Paul actually penned both 1 and 2 Thessalonians (2 Thessalonians 3:17), who does he include in the greetings (1 Thessalonians 1:1; 2 Thessalonians 1:1)? What kinds of pronouns does he use throughout his writing? What does this reveal about Paul's leadership style?

10. After Paul identifies the senders, he identifies the recipients with a profound statement (1:1). What do you think he means when he says the Thessalonians are "in" God the Father and the Lord Jesus Christ? How do the passages below help us understand this concept?

Colossians 3:3

Already within twenty years of the death and resurrection of Jesus the coupling of the Father and the Son as equal is the universal faith of the church. This simple fact is enough to undermine the teaching of those who claim that the New Testament nowhere attributes deity to Jesus.
—John Stott (*Message of 1 and 2 Thessalonians*, 27)

John 15:1, 5

DIGGING DEEPER

In 1 Corinthians 13:13, Paul lists three treasured ideas related to Christianity: faith, hope, and love. He also says that love is the greatest of the three. In your opinion, why is love the greatest?

11. What relationships or organizations are you "in" that have impacted your life? How do they pale compared to being "in" God the Father and the Lord Jesus Christ? What do you think this means?

12. Specifically, why do Paul and his companions thank God for the Thessalonian believers (1:1–3)?

13. Read 1:4–10 carefully again. Pay particular attention to what happened in the past to make them a flourishing church, how they were living out their faith in the present, and what they anticipated in the future that helped them persevere. Fill in the chart below with your observations:

Past	Present	Future
Paul came with words empowered by the Spirit.	They are imitating Paul and Jesus.	

14. What helped the Thessalonians persevere through extreme suffering (1:6)? What resulted (1:7–8)?

15. From what you know about the founding of the church in Acts 17, what kinds of challenges do you think the Thessalonians might have been forced to endure after Paul left?

16. What has helped you endure challenges in your life? What has resulted?

17. Many scholars believe Paul was only in Thessalonica for three short weeks. Yet in verse 7 he calls the baby Christians there "a model to all the believers." If Paul was writing a letter to you today, in what ways could he say that you are "a model" to others?

Thessalonica was in the province of Macedonia, while Corinth, where Paul resided when writing the letter, was in the province of Achaia.

DIGGING DEEPER

In verse 4, Paul reminds the Thessalonian brothers and sisters that God has chosen them to believe and become part of his forever family (την ἐκλογην ὑμων [*tēn eklogēn humōn*]). Jesus used the same term when he chose the twelve disciples (John 15:16). This Christian doctrine is called "election." Research this concept and explain how theologians attempt to understand the seeming conflict between election and our free will. An excellent resource is the classic little book *Evangelism and the Sovereignty of God* by J. I. Packer.

18. What are some practical ways you can help your church community gain a reputation of loving other churches in the area? How does being a model to others influence nonbelievers?

19. Chapter 1 ends with an important statement overflowing with meaning. We don't want to miss a single concept. Let's put the sentence under a magnifying glass to see what we can glean.

They tell how you turned to God from idols to serve the living and true God, and to wait for his Son from heaven, whom he raised from the dead—Jesus, who rescues us from the coming wrath (1:9–10).

Who is "they"? Who is "you"? Write their names above the words.

What do you learn about many of the Thessalonians' former religion?

Underline the verbs that signify what the Thessalonians are doing.

Which part of the statement refers to the present?

Which part of the statement reflects the future?

Who raised Jesus? _____

Who rescues us? _____

In light of the context, what do you think the word "wrath" means?

20. Does the idea of a resurrected Jesus returning fill you with hope and excitement? If so, why? If not, why not?

For in this hope we were saved. But hope that is seen is no hope at all. Who hopes for what they already have? But if we hope for what we do not yet have, we wait for it patiently.
—Romans 8:24–25

21. How do you think the Thessalonians knew that Jesus would return? Has anyone ever told you what the Bible says about your future? Discuss what you've been taught and your current thinking on the topic of "heaven" and our eternal destiny as Christians.

22. Why do you think God includes topics like "end times" in his Love Letter to you?

Paul's letters to the Thessalonians shed abundant light on what the Bible says about end times, more than any other biblical literature except the book of Revelation. As we journey through these letters, you'll have the opportunity to discern for yourself what you think about these important issues. It's the trip of a lifetime, so let's journey together.

The Prominent Women

by Misty Hedrick

Beloved, chosen
Valiant, voracious victors
Like dynamite, the Word exploded
Inside you
Spirit-ignited rockets, whistling higher
Lighting up night's raven clouds
Glittering, graceful, golden
Fast flared out, reverberant
Booming beyond the limits of your sky
Despite your open wounds—
Intended not only to beat,
But couldn't kill you—
Still you
Embodied our message with inexorable joy
You gripped the baton from Paul's hand
And ran,
Your idols fallen, left eating dust
Lungs screaming, hearts streaming
You ran just like us
Imitation, with no need for flattery
And now,
You too will turn the world upside down.

The Family Way | LESSON 2

Twenty years ago, when I taught a Bible study on God the Father, we surveyed the women participants and found that only about one in four grew up in a healthy family. I grieved that I wasn't one of them, as did many others. I suspect if we redid the survey, today the percentage would be even lower.

We each experience different family dynamics. Some enjoy large family gatherings, although size doesn't guarantee vitality. Others find holidays excruciatingly lonely with no one to celebrate with. And just because your family times might be rich today doesn't mean they will be tomorrow. Children grow up, move away, and create families of their own. Siblings distance. Parents and grandparents pass away.

Jesus knew we would all suffer from hunger for family—a place where we are cherished and can be ourselves. And he knew few would find that hunger met in this fallen world, so he established a new family, a forever family, for his people. The church. This family isn't perfect either, but one day it will be, and if we follow him well, the church can, and should, satisfy much of our current family hunger. Does your church feel like a family? Do you minister to one another like a thriving family would? Do you call yourselves family names? Jesus did.

> While Jesus was still talking to the crowd, his mother and brothers stood outside, wanting to speak to him. Someone told him, "Your mother and brothers are standing outside, wanting to speak to you."
>
> He replied to him, "Who is my mother, and who are my brothers?" Pointing to his disciples, he said, "Here are my mother and my brothers. For whoever does the will of my Father in heaven is my brother and sister and mother." (Matthew 12:46–50)

Jesus wasn't negating the importance of our families of origin, but he was accentuating the greater value of our spiritual families. The first is temporary, the second eternal.

OPTIONAL

Memorize 1 Timothy 5:1–2
Do not rebuke an older man harshly, but exhort him as if he were your father. Treat younger men as brothers, older women as mothers, and younger women as sisters, with absolute purity.

Who does Jesus include in the list of family members that was not mentioned before? Sisters! Women are included in Jesus' family! That might seem like a small thing to some, but to the marginalized women in the first century, this was tantamount to words of life. And they are still words of life to women today.
—Sue Edwards,
Kelley Mathews, and
Henry J. Rogers
(*Mixed Ministry*, 46)

Although Paul didn't have biological children, he and his companions model what a wholesome family looks like in his first letter to the Thessalonians. And he admonishes all of us to intentionally create similar dynamics in our local churches. Every one of us can belong to a hunger-busting family—if we all do our part.

 ## Read 1 Thessalonians 2.

Chapter 2 begins, "You know, brothers and sisters, that our visit to you was not without results." Some of your Bibles may only reference "brothers," but the Greek word here is *adelphoi*. It's a general term referring to all believers, both men and women. Without using the correct Greek term here, we'll easily miss Paul's emphasis on the family of God, a theme throughout much of this chapter and the whole New Testament.

DEALING WELL WITH OPPOSITION

1. Paul begins by reminding the Thessalonians of the outrageous treatment he experienced in Philippi right before he first visited Thessalonica and how God enabled him to boldly share the gospel with them despite strong opposition (2:2). How do you think you would have responded if you had been Paul? Why? How do you typically react when you believe you've failed? How do you think Paul would counsel you?

2. List at least three things Paul and his companions did not do during their time with the Thessalonians (2:3–6).

Instead of pressing on to Thessalonica from Philippi, Paul and Silas could have turned around and headed to port, setting sail back to Antioch with their scars of defeat still throbbing. They could have felt disqualified or at least unqualified by the rejection they had received. . . . But instead they knew something great leaders learn sooner or later: Disabilities need not disqualify.
—Charles Swindoll
(*1 & 2 Thessalonians*, 20)

We are hard pressed on every side, but not crushed; perplexed, but not in despair; persecuted, but not abandoned; struck down, but not destroyed.
—2 Corinthians 4:8–9

DIGGING DEEPER

To learn more about the experiences of Paul, Silas, and Timothy before traveling to Thessalonica, research what happened to them in Philippi (Acts 16:6–40). How did God use these horrific circumstances to birth the Philippian church, the first church founded on Paul's second missionary journey? Dissect the chapter carefully, and draw out insightful principles to help believers find joy in the midst of persecution and turmoil. What do you learn that you can apply to your own life today?

3. Why do you think Paul felt he needed to defend his motives and his conduct?

4. In an attempt to persuade or impress others, can you recall a time when you gave in to any of the temptations Paul resisted in 2:3–6? If so, which ones and why? How can you overcome these temptations?

FOCUS ON OUR FOREVER FAMILY

To live out our faith, we need the enabling supernatural strength God provides through the Holy Spirit, but we also need the support, care, and accountability of a forever family, our church.

In this section of the letter, Paul paints a picture of that ideal family by showing us how he and his companions treated the Thessalonians during his visit.

5. How did Paul describe his place in the family (2:7a)? What do you think he was attempting to communicate with this terminology? Why do you think this might have surprised the Thessalonians?

Remember the riots and legal charges that caused Paul and his fellow workers to flee at night. John Stott argues that Paul's enemies used his sudden disappearance to discredit him by saying, "He's just one more of those many phony teachers who tramp up and down the Egnatian Way. In a word, he's a charlatan. He's in this job only for what he can get . . . he doesn't care about you Thessalonian disciples of his; he has abandoned you!" (*Message of 1 and 2 Thessalonians*, 45–46).

A nationally known evangelist who preaches often about sexual morality is discovered to have a long-term relationship with a prostitute. . . . An investigation reveals that an evangelist-healer who claims to receive messages from God about people in his audience is actually being fed information by a colleague in a control room via a radio transmitter. And so on . . .
—Michael Holmes
(*1 & 2 Thessalonians*, 75)

Childhood was viewed primarily as a preparation and training for adult life. The Greco-Roman world had a high infant mortality rate, and due to overpopulation, babies, particularly girls, were often exposed. The newborn was not considered part of the family until acknowledged by the father as his child and received into the family in a religious ceremony, which meant they did not see exposure as infanticide but the refusal to admit to society. Some exposed babies were picked up by slave traders to be raised as slaves or prostitutes. Jewish and Christian laws prohibited this practice.
—Everett Ferguson
(*Backgrounds of Early Christianity*, 80–81)

6. In what sense is Paul asking us to emulate children? How might the passages below offer suggestions?

Psalm 8:1–2

Matthew 11:25

Matthew 18:1–5

1 John 3:1–3

7. Next Paul uses a maternal metaphor to describe his care for the Thessalonians (2:8). What words come to mind as you think about the deep personal relationship between a nursing baby and mother? Specifically, what did Paul and his companions do to illustrate this maternal metaphor among these baby believers? How can you imitate Paul?

8. In 2:9, Paul addresses the Thessalonians as brothers and sisters. Name some specific ways men and women can live out sacred sibling love in their relationships as brothers and sisters in the church. (See also 2:10.)

9. Paul continues his portrait of an ideal church family with a paternal metaphor. How did he deal with each Thessalonian believer (2:11–12)? How might you follow his example with people in your church family today?

10. What is another characteristic of a church that functions as a flourishing, wholesome family (2:13)? Why is this necessary for the long-term health of the church body?

DIGGING DEEPER

The Scriptures contain other examples of female and maternal pictures and metaphors: For example, investigate the contrast in Proverbs between chapter 5 and chapters 8 and 9. See also Psalm 91:1–6. What do these images teach us?

At first it is natural for a baby to take its mother's milk without knowing its mother. It is equally natural for us to see the man who helps us without seeing Christ behind him. But we must not remain babies. We must go on to recognize the real Giver.
—C. S. Lewis
(*Mere Christianity*, 163)

For a more thorough discussion on question 8, read *Mixed Ministry: Working Together as Brothers and Sisters in an Oversexed Society* by Sue Edwards, Kelley Mathews, and Henry J. Rogers.

When you sanitize your testimony and take out the hard parts you will forget about what God delivered you from.
—Jada Edwards
(IF:Lead 2019)

First Thessalonians 2:16 ends with a phrase that can be translated two ways:

"The wrath of God has come upon them at last" or "the wrath of God is over their heads." According to theologian John R. W. Stott, if the former, Paul may be referring to past events like the horrendous Judean famine of AD 45–47, the brutal massacre of Jews in the temple in AD 49 as described by historian Josephus, or when the emperor Claudius expelled the Jews from Rome. If the latter, Paul may be referring to end times events (*Message of 1 and 2 Thessalonians*, 55–59).

For insight on the term "coming wrath," see page 112 in the "Handy Glossary of End Times Terms."

DIGGING DEEPER

In 2:17, the word translated "to be orphaned" (*aporphanisthentes*) only occurs here in the entire New Testament. Look at this phrase in several different translations. Why do you think Paul used this word here to express his relationship with his Thessalonian brothers and sisters?

In 2:14–16, Paul mentions the Christians in Judea who were also persecuted by the Jewish leaders. He was referring to the first Christian church, pastored by Jesus's brother James. This church began in Jerusalem, located in the region of Judea, and soon other Judean churches probably sprang up in surrounding areas.

However, after Jewish leaders persecuted believers unmercifully, culminating in the stoning of Stephen (Acts 7:8–8:1), Christians scattered. But what their enemies meant for destruction, God used to spread Christianity throughout the known world.

From 2:14, we can infer that Paul and his companions shared stories of the bravery of the Judean Christians, which inspired the Thessalonians and other believers. The lesson for us? Tell your story. What God has done for you, he will use to encourage others who desperately need hope-filled models to follow.

11. Paul returns to his family metaphors in 2:17. What word does Paul use to describe how he felt when he was forced to leave the Thessalonians? What do you think he's attempting to communicate by using this word?

12. Summarize the various family-related characteristics Paul and his companions modeled for this newborn church in 2:7–12.

13. Some churches feel more like healthy families than others. Without mentioning names, what hinders churches from becoming the kind of church Paul modeled for the Thessalonians?

14. How can you make your church feel and interact more like a healthy family?

15. Paul laments that regardless of his intense desire, he hadn't been able to return to visit the Thessalonians because "Satan blocked our way" (2:18). From what you know about Paul and the circumstances he was facing, what might be some reasons he was not able to make a return visit?

> He [Paul] looked forward to the glad day when this life's journey would be over and he would be in the presence of the Lord along with all other Christians. Paul was picturing the rapture of the church, when Christ will come for His own to take them home to glory and all believers will appear before the judgment seat of Christ to receive reward or loss of reward (2 Cor. 5:10).
> —John F. Walvoord and Mark Hitchcock (*1 & 2 Thessalonians*, 45)

16. Let's wring out verses 19 and 20 to ensure we don't miss any of their inspiring truths.

For what is our hope, our joy, or the crown in which we will glory in the presence of our Lord Jesus when he comes? Is it not you? Indeed, you are our glory and joy.

Paul asks two rhetorical questions. What are they?

What words does Paul use to describe the Thessalonians and you? See also Philippians 4:1. Which words seem to relate to the present? Which seem to relate to the future?

DIGGING DEEPER

Tackle the fascinating study of believers receiving crowns as rewards in the New Testament. First, consider what 1 Corinthians 9:25 and Revelation 3:11–12 and 4:9–11 reveal about these future crowns. Second, consider the different crowns, what their names might signify, and who will receive them according to 2 Timothy 4:7–8, James 1:12, 1 Peter 5:2–4, and Revelation 2:10.

DIGGING DEEPER

In chapters 1 and 2, Paul has referred to our future destiny as believers three times:

"[You] wait for his Son from *heaven*, whom he raised from the dead— Jesus, who rescues us from *the coming wrath*" (1:10).

"[We were] urging you to live lives worthy of God, who calls you into his *kingdom and glory*" (2:12).

"For what is our hope, our joy, or the *crown in which we will glory in the presence of our Lord Jesus when he comes*?" (2:19).

To understand Paul's meaning, define the italicized terms above. For help, see the "Handy Glossary of End Times Terms" on pages 111–115. What can you learn about your future from the three passages above?

In what sense were believers Paul's "hope"? What do you think this word means in this context?

In what sense were believers Paul's "joy"? What do you think this word means in this context?

Paul also calls them his "crown." When will he have the opportunity to "glory" in them as his crown?

Paul uses the plural pronoun "our." How does that word change the meaning for Paul, for his companions, and for us?

Are you anyone's hope, joy, and crown? Is anyone yours? If so, who?

Child

by Misty Hedrick

I see you, God, as Father, kind,
though sometimes hard to read
beyond the boundaries still I find
your love for me, I need.

A fence cuts deep when tangled so
like barbed wire in my skin—
this wayward child you wrangle though,
with healing discipline.

I forfeit—I don't run the race
this wanderlust in me,
but you set lines in pleasant place
to save, and set me free.

Defend, protect, in me delight,
the apple of your eye,
strong champion, for me you fight,
deliverer on high.

And when I stray down pathways wild,
you plead my plight, my pain,
you watch for this prodigal child,
then sprint straight down the lane.

It's diff'rent with a mother's care:
you pull me gently tight,
you hold me close and stroke my hair—
sing o'er me in the night.

A mother cheers her children bold,
with heart that treasures stories,
you always lead me to behold
Jesus and his glories.

You bend to feed me, hold my hands,
you help me walk, break falls,
you hold me up with gentle bands,
make tender beck'ning calls.

I don't know who God is to you:
a friend? Or Father? Mother?
I do know this: God loves you too—
Christ . . . Savior, like no other.

How to Live Out Family Love | LESSON 3

OPTIONAL

Memorize 1 John
4:19–21

We love because he first
loved us. Whoever claims
to love God yet hates a
brother or sister is a liar.
For whoever does not love
their brother and sister,
whom they have seen,
cannot love God, whom
they have not seen. And
he has given us this com-
mand: Anyone who loves
God must also love their
brother and sister.

Your young son goes off to camp for the first time, or your beloved baby sister, daughter, or friend travels abroad for her first semester of college. Imagine all sources of communication are down and you've heard nothing from your loved one for weeks. Are they safe? Is some unscrupulous person taking advantage of them? Are they eating their vegetables? You lie awake at night, scary scenarios playing in your head. You feel concerned and helpless.

Although Paul spent a short time with the Thessalonians, he loved them like we love our dearest family and friends. Scholars debate exactly how long he spent in Thessalonica before he was forced to flee. Some say just the three weeks he preached in the Jewish synagogue (Acts 17:2–3). Others say he stayed longer, living in Jason's home and ministering to these new believers, who, like dry sponges, were eager to learn all they could. But no scholar suggests Paul was there more than a year. However long his stay, he left behind vulnerable baby Christians.

Like children away at camp for the first time or students attending their first semester of college in a foreign country, Paul wondered how they would fare, especially if they encountered opposition or danger. We can relate. We also dread being parted from loved ones, but Paul shows us how to weather the separation, how to encourage and interact with them despite the distance, and even how to find joy during our time apart. After all, for believers it's only temporary.

❧ Read 1 Thessalonians 3.

Paul yearned to visit his Thessalonian brothers and sisters, but returning was dangerous and would cause his new friend Jason to lose the bond he had posted (Acts 17:6–8)—so Paul sent Timothy.

1. How did Paul identify Timothy? What was Paul's twofold purpose in sending him (3:2)? How would you go about accomplishing these two tasks if you were Timothy?

> I believe in the immeasurable power of love; that true love can endure any circumstance and reach across any distance.
> —Steve Maraboli
> (*Unapologetically You*, 171)

2. How can you encourage and serve loved ones even when you are not together?

3. Specifically, why was Paul concerned for his beloved Thessalonians (3:3–5)? Do you share these kinds of concerns for those dear to you when they are far away? What did Paul model for us to help us love them well?

HOW TO RESPOND WELL WHEN PERSECUTED OR ENDURING HARDSHIPS

> No one goes sadly, reluctantly into discipleship with Jesus. As he said, "No one who looks back after putting his hand to the plough is suited to the kingdom of God" (Luke 9:62). No one goes in bemoaning the cost. They understand the opportunity.
> —Dallas Willard
> (*Divine Conspiracy*, 320)

4. During his stay, Paul taught them to expect persecution and hardships because of their faith. Why do you think it's important that Christians are made aware of this reality?

5. Why is it easy to be tempted to abandon your faith in the midst of suffering? See the list of natural but flawed responses to trials below. Check any that reflect your typical thinking patterns when life gets hard.

___ God doesn't love me.

___ I know God can do anything. But why won't he do this for me?

___ I am not worth it.

___ I have done something to deserve this.

___ Other Christians are so perfect. I keep messing up. I must not be a good Christian.

___ I've been burned too many times to keep showing up.

___ Numbing out isn't good for me, but it helps me survive.

___ God is mad at me and is punishing me.

___ I tried to be a good Christian and it didn't work.

___ That minister gave me bad advice. It's his/her fault.

___ I know _____ isn't good for me, but it helps.

Any ideas about why you tend to think this way? Why are these ideas flawed and harmful?

Instead of thinking about your struggles as described in the previous list, consider these alternative perspectives. Have you ever adopted any of the thinking patterns in the list below? Why are they far superior to the previous list?

___ God will use this to build my strength through this trial.

___ God saw my heart was too much set on being comfortable, and he intends to show me what is in my heart.

___ God saw that if this continued, I would fall into sin, so that the better my worldly situation, the worse for my soul, and he desired to save me from this calamity.

___ God intends to use my situation as a means to show himself mighty.

___ God intends to prepare me for some future work he has for me.

___ God wants to give me a platform to encourage others to believe in Jesus for their personal salvation.

Therefore, there is now no condemnation for those who are in Christ Jesus. . . . Who shall separate us from the love of Christ? Shall trouble or hardship or persecution or famine or nakedness or danger or sword? . . . No, in all these things we are more than conquerors through him who loved us. For . . . neither angels nor demons, neither the present nor the future, nor any powers, neither height nor depth, nor anything else in all creation, will be able to separate us from the love of God that is in Christ Jesus our Lord.
—Romans 8:1, 35, 37–39

Timothy met Paul at Corinth (Acts 18:5) and gave him the glad news that things were going well in Thessalonica. The phrase "brought us good tidings" is the exact equivalent of "preaching the Good News of the Gospel." The report was, to Paul, like hearing the Gospel.
—Warren Wiersbe (*Bible Exposition Commentary*, 172)

6. Paul writes this letter soon after Timothy returns from his trip to Thessalonica to discern how they are doing. What report does Timothy bring back (3:6–7)?

In spite of the stress of his circumstances and anxiety about the future, he [Paul] could take a deep breath and smile at the thought that his spiritual children in Thessalonica would be just fine. Though Satan had put the squeeze on their earthly comfort, God's spiritual truths brought an inexplicable strength, peace, and joy. Paul knew that nobody could force the Thessalonians to flee from their faith. Christ Himself had invaded that city. And he was there to stay.
—Charles Swindoll (*1 & 2 Thessalonians*, 39)

7. What effect does Timothy's report have on Paul (3:8–9)?

8. How do you think it's possible to experience the kinds of trials, persecution, and discomfort that Paul lived with daily and still say, "Now [I] really live" (verse 8)?

In 3:10 Paul reiterates how much he longs to see the Thessalonians again. One reason is so he can "supply what is lacking in your faith." Paul isn't rebuking them for their lack of faith but wishing he could be there to continue teaching them in person, to fill the gaps in their instruction.

9. What do you need to "really live"?

10. This section of the letter ends with a benediction in the form of a prayer and serves to summarize his writing so far (3:11–13). What are Paul's three main requests?

A benediction is a proclamation of God's blessings on someone. A prominent example is the great priestly blessing in Numbers 6:24–26. Many New Testament letters close with benedictions, including Romans 15:13, 2 Corinthians 13:14, and Hebrews 13:20–21.

🌸 **Read 1 Thessalonians 4:1–12.**

Next Paul gets specific regarding what he meant in 3:13 when he called the Thessalonians and us to become "blameless and holy."

11. Do you think it's possible to ever become completely "blameless and holy" in this life? Why or why not? What's Paul suggesting in 4:1–2?

In 3:13 Paul prays the Thessalonians will be strong in faith so they "will be blameless and holy in the presence of our God and Father when our Lord Jesus comes with all his holy ones." I believe he refers to the rapture. Jesus is taking us to heaven at the rapture and bringing us back to earth with him later to be with him when he sets up his millennial kingdom.

12. Paul sets before the Thessalonians two life paths: sexual immorality or sexual purity (3:13; 4:1–5). Why was it especially difficult to live a pure life in Thessalonica?

Scholar John Walvoord also argues for the rapture in 3:13: "According to Scripture, Christians are going to meet Christ in the air. We are going to be present with Him at that moment. After we meet Him in the air, He will take us home to glory to be in the presence of the Father and the holy angels. . . . When the dead in Christ and living Christians are caught up to be with the Lord and arrive in heaven as the trophies of grace, the marvels of God's resurrection power, they will be presented as a spotless bride, as a holy people, as those who are the workmanship of Christ. At the coming of Christ with all His saints to heaven, we will be 'unblameable in holiness before God, even our Father'" (*Thessalonian Epistles*, 33–34).

DIGGING DEEPER

How does 1 John 3:2–3 relate to verse 13?

A real Person, Christ, here and now, in that very room where you are saying your prayers, is doing things to you. It is not a question of a good man who died two thousand years ago. It is a living Man, still as much a man as you, and still as much God as He was when He created the world, really coming and interfering with your very self; killing the old natural self in you and replacing it with the kind of self He has. At first, only for moments. Then for longer periods. Finally, if all goes well, turning you permanently into a different sort of thing; into a new little Christ, a being which, in its own small way, has the same kind of life as God; which shares in His power, joy, knowledge and eternity.
—C. S. Lewis
(*Mere Christianity*, 164)

Many of us hear the word *purity* and think *that could never be me*, and we check out of the conversation. We might feel that we could never be pure either because of others' actions against us or our own bad choices. But remember that Paul's words urge purity going forward. As DTS professor Dr. Sandra Glahn said to a student, "Purity is yielded—it cannot be taken." What someone else did to us in the past was not our fault. What we chose to do in the past, Christ already forgave. From now on, in the strength of the Spirit, choose to walk in purity."

13. Whether you are married, single, single again, or widowed, sexual temptation is everywhere in most modern-day cultures. What causes you to struggle with sexual purity today? If you have found ways to take the path of purity, share those strategies with the group.

14. What is Paul's command in 4:6a? What are some ways Christians might take advantage or wrong a brother or sister sexually in the family of God?

15. How can Christians take Paul's command in verse 4:6a seriously without destroying the family atmosphere required for health in the Body of Christ? How do biological families accomplish this (1 Timothy 5:1–2)?

16. In the latter part of verse 6, Paul tells us that there are serious consequences for living an immoral life. Why is this sin so serious (4:7–8)? What kinds of consequences have you witnessed or experienced?

17. Paul praised the Thessalonians because they not only loved their brothers and sisters in their own church well, but they had somehow expressed their love to churches all over the region (4:9–10). Can you think of ways this young church might have gained this reputation?

18. What are meaningful and tangible ways you can love Christians in other churches? Why do you think Paul was so pleased with these actions and attitudes? How did this promote the gospel?

> Therefore, my dear friends, as you have always obeyed—not only in my presence, but now much more in my absence—continue to work out your salvation with fear and trembling, for it is God who works in you to will and to act in order to fulfill his good purpose.
> —Paul to the Philippians (Philippians 2:12–13)

> I think too often churches either avoid the topic or settle for an unbiblical "strategy of isolation" where men deliberately separate themselves from women as a means of temptation avoidance. This leads to a loss of biblical community, lost opportunities for the development of leadership gifts, and doesn't even help in avoiding sin. For God's intent is that we aim at becoming the kind of persons who treat one another as brother and sister.
> —John Ortberg (quoted in Sue Edwards, Kelley Mathews, and Henry J. Rogers, *Mixed Ministry*, 28)

Paul also admonished the Thessalonians to love outsiders through the way they conducted their everyday lives.

19. What do you think Paul means in 4:11 when he says the following?

Lead a quiet life.

The final issue here (vv. 11–12) is debated but likely stems from a group who stopped working and contributing to society but just sat back waiting for the Lord to return and allowing the rest of the "shallower" Christians who were working to take care of them. They had become selfish busybodies and were turning the community around them against the church due to their selfishness and lack of love. They were losing the respect of the unbelievers and were disrupting the peace and sanctity of the church. Paul urges the saints there to solve the dilemma and turn their whole congregation into trustworthy contributors to those around.
—Grant Osborne
(*1 & 2 Thessalonians*, 102)

Mind your own business.

"Make it your ambition to lead a quiet life" seems like a paradox; if you are ambitious, your life will probably not be quiet. But the emphasis is on quietness of mind and heart, the inner peace that enables a man to be sufficient through faith in Christ. Paul did not want the saints running around creating problems as they earned their daily bread.
—Warren Wiersbe (*Bible Exposition Commentary*, 177)

Work with your hands (be self-supporting).

Which of these mandates is most difficult for you? Why?

20. Instead, how do some of today's cultures encourage us to do the opposite?

21. Why does Paul suggest we live this way (4:12)?

22. How would your life change if you took Paul's mandate in 4:11 seriously? What changes in actions and attitudes would be a helpful starting point?

What does Paul mean when he instructs us to "not be dependent on anybody" (4:12)? Is he contradicting his previous teaching that believers are family and must encourage, comfort, and help one another? No, Paul's direction in Galatians 6:1–6 provides some insight. In verse 2 he writes, "Carry each other's burdens," but in verse 5 he says, "Each one should carry their own load." A burden is a load that's so heavy that the individual cannot carry it alone. Brothers and sisters must come alongside to help. But it's equally true that we must not be lazy and fail to each do our part so we don't take advantage of a brother or sister. This breeds resentment, disagreements, and ultimately disunity. Paul will talk more about some Thessalonians' failure to bear their own load in his second letter.   —Sue

The watching world is not hugely impressed by emotional hype and extremism, but is attracted by ordinary people, living ordinary lives, who demonstrate an extraordinary godliness, seen in love.
—David Jackman
(*Authentic Church*, 111)

Parting

by Misty Hedrick

I looked into your flooded eyes,
Wounded, saying our goodbyes
Heart-shredded friendship
Torn away, souls strip
Cracked open
For you.
In Athens all alone I stayed
Bursting love for you, I prayed
Spoken syllables to God
Flung off my tongue, hit roughshod
Endlessly
For you.
I knew my destiny—Rome chained
Rod-beaten corpse, still unashamed
Stoned and bloody, crushed unjust
Breathless lying in the dust
But I rise up
For you.
Powerless to carry the weight secure,
Desperate to know if you stood sure.
Our hunger too long left unsated
We sent Timothy, and waited
Lonely
For you.
Good news, flaming, unextinguished
Shared, suffered certain faith—distinguished
Together, blameless, we press toward
Holy eyes focused, beaming forward
Hopeful we watch
For him.

I'll Fly Away | LESSON 4

What happens when we die? Death haunts many people so much that they block out its existence and refuse to admit it's real. They can't talk about it. They find excuses not to attend funerals. They neglect visiting loved ones on their deathbeds. I remember a close family member refused to see his mother before she died, saying, "I'd rather remember her the way she was," ignoring her request to see her son one last time.

In his Love Letter, God reveals what happens when we die, but the pieces are spread out like a puzzle, and we must put the pieces together. Maybe he expects we will read it all and work the puzzle, or maybe he doesn't want us overwhelmed—as seeing the whole picture at once might do.

Before I trusted Christ as my personal Savior, I was terrified of dying. Now, in my later years I'm more at peace, although I don't look forward to the process. As one of my professor colleagues says, "I'm asking Jesus for a face plant." When the time comes, I'd like to just drop dead too, but it's out of my hands and out of yours.

Obviously, in the brief time Paul spent discipling the Thessalonians, he taught them some basics about their eternal future—about a time when Jesus said, "I will come back and take you to be with me that you may also be where I am" (John 14:3).

These new exuberant believers expected Jesus would come for them right away. But since Paul's quick departure, some of their loved ones had died, and those left behind wondered if Jesus would come for their dearly departed too. Timothy relayed their concern to Paul, and Paul addressed their questions in this letter.

I'm grateful Paul did, because these revelations are encouraging sources of hope for all of us who claim the name of Christ and yearn for his reappearing.

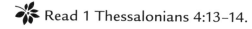 Read 1 Thessalonians 4:13–14.

OPTIONAL

Memorize John 14:1–3

Do not let your hearts be troubled. You believe in God; believe also in me. My Father's house has many rooms; if that were not so, would I have told you that I am going there to prepare a place for you? And if I go and prepare a place for you, I will come back and take you to be with me that you also may be where I am.

Have you been to a funeral where someone says, "Well, they're in a better place now" in response to the raw emotion of the moment? Do those kinds of words short-circuit the grieving process? Study the responses of Mary, Martha, and Jesus to the death of Lazarus (John 11:1–43). What are some of the principles there that instruct Christians in a healthy response to the death of a loved one?

Preachers shout, "Where is your sting, O death?" just inches away from an occupied casket. I always want to shout back, "It's right there! There's the sting!" Do you see in 1 Corinthians 15 when death loses its sting? Do you see when it's swallowed up in victory and can no longer create mourning? It is when we put on the imperishable. So, at funerals we mourn and we hurt; death stings, and there is real loss. This text rightly used at a funeral should point us to the hope of the day where it won't sting any longer.
—Matt Chandler
(*Explicit Gospel*, Kindle loc. 2563)

1. From verse 13, how were the Thessalonians probably reacting to the deaths of their loved ones?

2. Why can we grieve in a different way than nonbelievers? Have you experienced this reality? If so, please share how being "informed" allowed you to grieve differently?

Now let's consider four questions Christians typically ask about death.

QUESTION ONE: WHAT HAPPENS WHEN WE DIE PHYSICALLY?

3. Where do we begin in our understanding of what happens when we die (4:14a)? Why is this the bedrock of our hope (1 Corinthians 15:12–20)? Do you believe this? Why or why not?

4. Let's dissect the second part of verse 14:

. . . and so we believe that God will bring with Jesus those who have fallen asleep in him.

What do you think the term "fallen asleep in him" means? When you fall asleep tonight, what is your reasonable expectation in the morning?

The object of the metaphor is to suggest that as the sleeper does not cease to exist while his body sleeps, so the dead person continues to exist despite his absence from the region in which those who remain can communicate with him, and that, as sleep is known to be temporary, so the death of the body will be found to be. Sleep has its waking, death will have its resurrection.
—C. F. Hogg and W. E. Vine
(*Epistles of Paul the Apostle to the Thessalonians*, 128)

How does Paul answer the Thessalonians' question about their loved ones who have died since Paul left?

In light of John 14:3, "I will come back and take you to be with me that you also may be where I am," what can we deduce?

Thus far, we know that Jesus is going to take us somewhere to be with him, but we don't know a number of details—exactly where is he taking us, and when, and what part of us goes with him? To answer these questions, we need to discover other pieces of the puzzle in other parts of the Bible. Let's answer these questions for the Thessalonians and then extrapolate these revelations for ourselves.

In 2 Corinthians 5, Paul explains what happens to a Christian's body and spirit when they die.

> For we know that if the earthly tent we live in is destroyed, we have a building from God, an eternal house in heaven, not built by human hands. (verse 1)

> Therefore we are always confident and know that as long as we are at home in the body we are away from the Lord . . . I say, and would prefer to be away from the body and at home with the Lord. (verses 6–9)

5. What does God call our physical body in verse 1? In what way is a building or a house superior to a tent? What happens to our "tent" when we die, according to verse 1?

6. Paul says when we inhabit our physical body, we are away from the Lord. In what sense is this true? What part of us leaves the physical body and is present with the Lord when we die physically?

7. Summarize what happened to the bodies and spirits of the Thessalonians' loved ones when they died, and what has happened to all believers, and will happen to us when/if we die physically.

QUESTION THREE: WHAT HAPPENS TO BELIEVERS WHO ARE ALIVE WHEN GOD BEGINS HIS TIMETABLE TO INAUGURATE HIS END TIMES PLAN?

 Read 1 Thessalonians 4:15–17.

In this passage, Paul explains God's dramatic kickoff to begin the count-down to the end of time as we know it—the rapture.

It's also helpful to see this event as the first of a two-part second com-ing. In the rapture Jesus returns to remove his beloved believers from the horrendous crises that will soon invade the earth. How like our loving God to show such marvelous mercy for his own. But it's important to note, his feet never touch down on the earth at the rapture. This means the rapture isn't the second coming—that will come later. This is just the opening bell to the end times.

8. What can you learn about the rapture from 4:15–17? Who does Jesus snatch away first in the rapture?

Since 2 Corinthians 5:6–9 tells us that the spiritual part of the dead are already with Jesus, what part of them rises at the rapture (see also 1 Corinthians 15:35, 42–44)?

What kind of fanfare will accompany the rapture?

> This "coming" (Gr. *parousia*, lit. "appearing") of Christ is the same as His appear-ing in the clouds (cf. Acts 1:11). It is not His Second Coming, following the Tribulation, a separate "coming"—at which time He will remain on the earth, set up His earthly kingdom, and reign for 1,000 years (cf. Rev. 19:11–21). The differences in the descrip-tions of these comings present them as separate events (cf. Matt. 24:30–31 and 1 Thess. 4:15–17).
> —Thomas Constable
> (*Notes on 1 Thessalonians*, 41)

What happens to those who are alive at the time of the rapture?

What blessing will all who are raptured enjoy forever?

1 Corinthians 15:51–53 provides more details about the changes we will experience at the rapture.

> Listen, I tell you a mystery: We will not all sleep, but we will all be changed—in a flash, in the twinkling of an eye, at the last trumpet. For the trumpet will sound, the dead will be raised imperishable, and we will be changed. For the perishable must clothe itself with the imperishable, and the mortal with immortality.

9. How fast will the rapture occur?

10. When the spiritual parts of the dead are reunited with their physical bodies, how do their physical bodies change?

There is no reference in the Old Testament to saints being raptured, taken from earth to heaven without dying. There are many references to Christ coming back to the earth and of resurrection from the dead, but no rapture, no translation in the Old Testament, except by way of illustration in the cases of Elijah and Enoch.
—John Walvoord
(*Thessalonian Epistles*, 49)

What's the difference between perishable and imperishable? Between mortal and immortal?

Following the rapture, the church will be in glory, but on earth the great climactic event of this age, the great tribulation, will rage. Yet even during that awful time the Lord will graciously call many Jews and Gentiles to trust in Christ (Rev. 7:1–18).
—John F. Walvoord and Mark Hitchcock (*1 & 2 Thessalonians*, 72)

11. According to 1 Corinthians 15:54–55, what will be one reason believers will all experience ecstatic celebration at the rapture? What difference should this truth make in your life right now?

QUESTION FOUR: WHAT IS THE DAY OF THE LORD?

 Read 1 Thessalonians 5:1–11.

The "day of the Lord" refers to a large number of dramatic end times events prophesied in both the Old and New Testaments. It includes both judgment (the tribulation) and blessing (Christ's millennial kingdom).

Old Testament prophets wrote about "that day":

Alas for that day! For the day of the LORD is near; it will come like destruction from the Almighty. (Joel 1:15)

Will not the day of the LORD be darkness, not light—pitch-dark, without a ray of brightness? (Amos 5:20)

The LORD will be king over the whole earth. On that day there will be one LORD, and his name the only name. (Zechariah 14:9)

The New Testament concurs:

But the day of the Lord will come like a thief. The heavens will disappear with a roar; the elements will be destroyed by fire, and the earth and everything done in it will be laid bare. (2 Peter 3:10)

But judgment is necessary—unless we are to conclude, absurdly, that nothing much is wrong, or, blasphemously, that God doesn't mind very much. . . . And this is of course the crunch—where those who have acted wickedly refuse to see the point, there can be no reconciliation, no embrace.
—N. T. Wright (*Surprised by Hope*, 179)

Today we live in the day of grace, also called the church age. Our salvation, through the sacrifice of Christ on the cross in our place, and our enablement to live the Christian life are entirely dependent on the grace and mercy of God. When Jesus raptures the church, taking her to the heavenly realms, the church age ends and the day of the Lord begins.

Apparently, just knowing about the day of the Lord caused the Thessalonians to ask specifically when the different end times events that Paul had taught them about would occur, including the day of the Lord. As naturally curious people, we would like to know dates and times too, so we can plan ahead.

12. How does Paul respond to their desire to know exact times in 5:1? What did Jesus say when the disciples wanted to know (Acts 1:6–8)?

13. Why do you think God chooses not to give us this information?

14. When Paul was with them, he had taught them about "the day of the Lord." What had he taught them about that day (5:2)?

15. Pay special attention to the pronouns Paul uses in 5:1–2 and 4–11 (we, you, us) in contrast to the noun and pronouns he uses in 5:3 (people, them, they). What does this switch in pronouns tell us?

16. Paul uses two metaphors to describe the nature of the day of the Lord. What are they (5:2–3)? What do you think these metaphors tell us about the day of the Lord? What will this mean for unbelievers who will endure the tribulation and other coming judgments once Jesus snatches the church away?

17. Why might Paul want the Thessalonians to know what's ahead for unbelievers? See also 2 Peter 3:8–9.

18. Next Paul contrasts believers with nonbelievers. What words describe believers? How are we to be different from those who don't know and love God? (5:4–7) What do you think he's attempting to communicate to the Thessalonians and to us?

The intention of the apostle is not merely to inform or debate but also to change the conduct of the Thessalonians, so that the fear they now experience over their own fate on the day of the Lord would be replaced with the comfort that comes from knowing their privileged status of being "sons of light/day" and their election by God not to face his wrath but to obtain salvation and eternal life with Christ.
—Jeffrey Weima
(*1–2 Thessalonians*, 339)

19. Specifically, how does Paul say a Christian lives a "sober" life (5:8)?

20. What's the main concept Paul wants the Thessalonians, and us, to grasp from this part of the letter (5:9–10)?

21. What's Paul's main purpose in telling us about God's great end times plan (5:11; 4:18)?

22. The expectancy that Christians hold in regard to the rapture in many theological circles is called "immanency," which means that nothing else needs to occur before Jesus returns to rapture his beloved people. As a result, Christians are called to be watchful, aware, attentive, and observant. What would it look like in your life right now if you were actively watching for the rapture? Would it look different in terms of how you relate to God? To other believers? To unbelievers?

Waiting for a Cloudy Day

by Misty Hedrick

Oh God, help me! I pray as salt crystals roll, flood
The night vise-gripped my heart—hold on till tomorrow.
Where hides the hope, the hope for which you shed your blood?

My soul cringed from lack of breathed hope to borrow,
Safe door tight-sealed alone, alone—Oh God, I grieved!—
As night dripped long, collapsed beneath toxic sorrow.

Victory over death he taught, and I believed
Yet beside carved-stone, sod-thrown, grass-grown pit I stood.
Now preach! Restore to me the gospel I received.

My loving Savior gazed down from his cross of wood,
Bruised knees, face drowned, back bowed—Oh how, God, do
    you save?
I pray, compel, dispel this hell—return for good!

At once I heard dawn's shined-brass bugler blare out brave,
Caught up in raptured hope-etched clouds, rise from the grave.

Live Out Your Glorious Hope | LESSON 5

Paul ends his letter with practical advice. In light of our glorious futures, here's how we should live. He begins by reminding us that we are family—spiritual brothers and sisters (5:12). But today, again, I saw a Christian bashing another Christian on social media. I'm not surprised when pagans without a moral compass set fires and spew hatred, but I grieve when I see similar hostility bleed into the local church when believers don't get their way. Sometimes that meanness is directed at one another, but more often it's directed at leaders. I've experienced it myself.

Like all families, we sometimes disagree and need to lovingly confront one another, but unless issues of essential doctrine or blatant sin are at stake, we are called to peace and unity for the sake of Christ's reputation. No one wins when the church family chews on one another instead of the Word.

Paul begins by advising us about how to treat church leaders.

❀ Read 1 Thessalonians 5:12–13.

1. How does God expect his people to treat their church leaders?

OPTIONAL

Memorize Hebrews 10:23

Let us hold unswervingly to the hope we profess, for he who promised is faithful.

God will never convict unless he fully intends to empower.
—Priscilla Shirer
(*Armor of God*, 90)

2. Why do you think this admonition is first on Paul's list? What unintended consequences can result from church family fights?

3. What's your attitude toward those God has put in positions of leadership in your church family?

4. What are your expectations of your church leaders? Considering that leaders are finite people just like you, are your expectations reasonable?

5. What do you do when you think your leader has made a poor decision or not lived up to your expectations?

6. How did Jesus teach us to handle valid disagreements with one another (Matthew 18:15–17)? What might that process look like between a church leader and a member of the local church body?

7. Have you ever followed, or failed to follow, the mandate of Matthew 18:15–17 with a fellow Christian? (No names, please.) What happened? What did you learn?

For a thorough treatment of how women do conflict, to hear how I followed and failed to follow Matthew 18:15–17 in a life-altering church conflict, and to equip yourself for inevitable disagreements, read my book *Leading Women Who Wound*, coauthored with Kelley Mathews.   —Sue

Read 1 Thessalonians 5:14–15.

In these two verses, we find rich instructions to help the church family love one another well, especially the needy or problem "children." Remember, the Thessalonians are young in the faith and facing severe persecution. Just like when any family is in crisis, the strong reach out and help struggling family members who need help. Grammatically, these verses contain five mandates. Let's look at each.

This word [disruptive, unruly] means "careless, out of line." It was applied to a soldier who would not keep rank but insisted on marching his own way. · . . .This kind of attitude in the church family causes arguments and splits.
—Warren Wiersbe
(*Be Ready*, 120–21)

MANDATE ONE: WARN THOSE WHO ARE IDLE AND DISRUPTIVE

8. What does it mean to be idle? Feel free to use a dictionary or concordance to help.

9. Why does idleness lead to disruptive behavior?

10. What do you think an idle lifestyle reveals about someone's character?

11. What does Paul recommend we do when we observe an idle Christian? What's a loving way to do this?

MANDATE TWO: ENCOURAGE THE DISHEARTENED

12. See the sidebar that explains the meaning of the Greek word translated here as "disheartened" or "timid." Do you know someone you think would fit this definition? If so, describe them. (No names, please.)

13. Why do you think the disheartened need special help from others in their church family?

14. Please share a time when you were disheartened and another believer encouraged you.

15. If you have been a "minister of encouragement," what have you learned that could benefit others?

We all know those who struggle under the weight of life's problems and get discouraged, afraid, and despondent more easily than others. . . . In this case the ministry of encouragement can be like a car with battery cables that comes alongside another car with a dead battery to give it a jump start, transfer of power. The Lord wants us to come alongside those who are discouraged and give them a spiritual jump start.
—John F. Walvoord and Mark Hitchcock
(*1 & 2 Thessalonians*, 100)

MANDATE THREE: HELP THE WEAK

Theologian Tom Constable describes the "weak" as those who had not yet learned dependence on the Lord for their needs, the spiritually "weak," and he suggested that they were worthy of special support (*Notes on 1 Thessalonians*, 76).

16. How might the Thessalonians have offered support for the "weak" through the crises they faced daily? How can you help those who are "weak" in your church family?

MANDATE FOUR: BE PATIENT WITH EVERYONE

17. What kinds of people in your church family "try your patience"? What is Paul asking you to do? Why?

MANDATE FIVE: DON'T PAY BACK WRONG FOR WRONG

18. What is your natural tendency when someone wrongs you?

19. What does Jesus advise us to do in Matthew 5:38–42?

20. Why is this strategy more likely to result in repentance and peace (Romans 12:20–21)?

✿ Read 1 Thessalonians 5:16–22.

In light of the reality that Jesus is coming back for us at any time, now Paul shares five ways to honor God, make him look good, and deepen our relationship with him as we wait.

21. What do each of the first three commands mean in your everyday life? Which is more difficult for you? Why?

Rejoice always.

Pray continually.

The concept communicated by the mandate to "pray continually" describes a person who continually clears their throat or suffers from a nagging cough. Charles Ryrie adds, "Just as a person with a hacking cough is not always audibly coughing though the tendency to cough is always there, so the Christian who prays without ceasing is not always praying audibly and yet prayer is always the attitude of his heart and life" ("First and Second Thessalonians," 80).

Give thanks in all circumstances; for this is God's will for you in Christ Jesus.

22. Obviously, Paul had taught them about the work of the Holy Spirit in their lives when he was with them before. Now he warns them: "Do not quench the Spirit."

What does it mean to "quench" something?

What are ways we can quench the Spirit in our lives?

What are we risking if we do?

23. In verses 20–21 Paul instructed the Thessalonian Christians not to believe everything they heard but to "test" or discern truth from error. As we listen to Bible preachers and teachers, how do we do that today?

❧ Read 1 Thessalonians 5:23–28.

What a beautiful farewell!

24. Imagine Paul peering into the imagined faces of his beloved Thessalonians and praying over them in verses 23–24. What does he pray for
them, and how will this be accomplished?

25. What does he ask in 5:25–26? Although these are specific requests,
what do you think he's generally requesting from them?

26. He ends his letter with a final blessing and an admonition to share this
letter with other believers. How can you do that today (5:27–28)?

27. Look back over this letter. What have you learned that you didn't
know before? Did anything surprise you, convict you, change your
thinking? What will you remember about Paul's first letter to the
Thessalonians in the future?

DIGGING DEEPER

In 5:17, Paul charges that
this letter be read to
everyone in the church. The
Greek word for "charge"
is *enorkizō* and is only
used here in Paul's letters.
Generally, this word is used
when someone requires
an oath in response to the
charge. Here, Paul uses this
word to communicate the
seriousness of this require-
ment. The guarantor of
the oath was "the Lord,"
who would be expected
to exact judgment if the
oath were not carried out.
Why do you think Paul
asks the Thessalonians
to enter into this pledge?
If you were a part of this
church, what would you do
to help fulfill this oath?

Some commentators have
understood Paul's reference
here to "spirit, soul, and
body," to be an indica-
tion that each person is
composed of three distinct
parts: the physical (body)
. . . the mental/emotional
(soul) . . . and the spiritual
(spirit) which relates to
God. . . . Complex theories
of salvation and sanctifica-
tion have developed around
this idea of the trichotomy
(or threefold nature) of
humans. . . . In any case,
the purpose of the passage
is not to establish a biblical
doctrine of the component
parts of a human person,
but to simply pray that
God would protect every
dimension of our lives.
—Charles Swindoll
(*1 & 2 Thessalonians*, 97)

A Job Well Done

by Misty Hedrick

I obeyed my father:
Worked as teacher, planter, and reaper,
A doctor, a lawyer, bridge builder, and barrier bomber
A fisherman, a true friend,
And a servant, scrubbing the feet of men
Who found me worthless—
My mind screamed against injustice
My work—flawless,
Yet in the garden I stood,
Praying, *Let this cup pass from me, please, if you could.*
Still wedged into this body I made
Soul scarred and a little afraid
Dismayed friends strayed—
But the women stayed.
Shivering, abandoned, abused
I didn't even count how many whips they used.
They tried to medicate, get me to extricate
With wine and gall, enticed
Their loss, my cross—
Above the toss of clattering dice
In rising wrathful gale, I turned pale.
Uncommitted sin—I'm all in.
Dying for you—doing what you couldn't do.
Who is God?
Is there not only one?
Where is God?
Why hasn't he come?
My soul reeled—
Because if anybody knew he was real,
It was me.
But there I hung on the tree.
I obeyed my father: saw it through till the end
Felt like relief when they took my body down again
Buried in a tomb they didn't know I owned
There I lay three days in the dark all alone.
But that third day—write this down, don't doubt—
Because on that third day—
I walked out.

2 THESSALONIANS

Beware of Tricksters

Memorize 2 Peter 2:1
But there were also false prophets among the people, just as there will be false teachers among you. They will secretly introduce destructive heresies, even denying the sovereign Lord who bought them—bringing swift destruction on themselves.

Many of us like to plan ahead so we know what to expect next, and we become agitated, vulnerable, and bewildered when faced with uncertainty. A continually postponed follow-up mammogram appointment. A pandemic that disrupts everything "normal" with no definite end date. An undiagnosed illness. A presumed layoff in a vacillating job market. The Thessalonians shared similar feelings, but for different reasons.

Earlier Paul had taught them that Jesus would return "soon"; they assumed probably during their lifetime. This event would usher in the "day of the Lord." This grand news filled them with jubilance, hope, and expectation. But he was forced to leave without an opportunity to fill in details or answer questions. During Paul's absence, some of their loved ones died and the Thessalonians had no idea what would happen to their dearly departed when Jesus returned for them. Their confusion made these new converts vulnerable to "wolves in sheepskins."

John Walvoord and Mark Hitchcock write: "The occasion for 2 Thessalonians was the receipt of the news that the Thessalonians had received a spurious letter, apparently an intentional forgery, teaching them that they were already in the day of the Lord and its awful judgments. . . . Paul penned this letter to correct this misunderstanding" (*1 & 2 Thessalonians*, 17).

Evidently this forged letter contradicted what Paul taught earlier about end times. This person or group may have emerged in person to stir up division or gain influence. Confused and disturbed, the Thessalonians wondered, "Are we children of darkness rather than light? And what about Grandma, who passed in her sleep, and Sarah, who died in childbirth?" They didn't know who to believe—Paul or these "new apostles." When Paul learned of this deception, he wrote 2 Thessalonians using rational arguments to set the record straight.

Also, some Thessalonians had quit their jobs and prepared to move to the mountaintop, waiting for the end. They misread their circumstances and foolishly misunderstood God's intent for revealing various aspects of our future. Unfortunately, it isn't just the Thessalonians who

One of the most profound contributions of this letter is the balanced perspective it brings to the subject of end-times prophecy. We ought to be neither passive and ignorant nor fanatical and extreme when it comes to either the big picture or the details of Christ's coming as Judge and King. Rather, we should be alert, aware of all the devilish deceptions around us, and confident in God's plan, living our Christian lives responsibly to the glory of God.
—Charles Swindoll
(*1 & 2 Thessalonians*, 103)

misunderstand the purpose (and timing) of the end times. Even today some Christians continue to be misled by quacks. Paul wrote this letter to warn us about them.

Are you vulnerable, easily persuaded by slick tricksters who delight in misleading believers who aren't firmly founded on God's Word? We would all do well to take to heart Jesus's words to his disciples just before he left the earth: "It is not for you to know the times or dates the Father has set by his own authority. But you will receive power when the Holy Spirit comes on you; and you will be my witnesses in Jerusalem, and in all Judea and Samaria, and to the ends of the earth" (Acts 1:7–8).

Jesus's parting words exhort us not to focus on timetables or wait on mountaintops for Jesus to snatch us away. Instead, both Jesus and Paul emphatically tell us where to expend our energies during our gift of days. Digest Paul's insightful second letter to the Thessalonians that reveals how we can protect ourselves from deception and live well in the wait.

❋ Read 2 Thessalonians 1.

1. The Thessalonians had only been believers for a short time. Nevertheless, what does Paul say about them in 1:3? Why might they have needed words of encouragement right then?

2. What do Paul's words of encouragement before later correction teach you about wise interaction with people?

3. What is Paul acknowledging about their circumstances (1:4)? Why do they need to hear this?

4. In 1:5 Paul informs the Thessalonians that God sees their suffering and perseverance in the face of increased hostility and will reward them at the proper time. Have you ever considered this truth in the midst of suffering? Why do you think God reveals this reality to us in the Bible?

5. In addition to rewarding his own, what else must God do because he is just (1:6, 8–9)? How do you feel about this divine truth?

6. In 1:8 Paul identifies unbelievers as "those who do not know God and do not obey the gospel of our Lord Jesus." The apostle John defines what it means to know God and to obey the gospel (1 John 5:10–12). What is the main thing that separates believers and unbelievers? How does God feel about unbelievers (2 Peter 3:8, 15; Matthew 23:37)?

In the thick of their suffering at the hands of the Jews on one side, Gentiles on the other, and teachers from within, the last thing the Thessalonians needed from Paul in the first paragraph was criticism. . . . Rather, they needed sustenance for the hard journey.
—Charles Swindoll
(1 & 2 Thessalonians, 114)

DIGGING DEEPER

Is Paul saying in 1:5 that the Thessalonians' ability to endure through trials is the reason they will live eternally as part of God's forever family? What does their ability to endure show? See 1 Peter 1:3–9.

There's a story of two farmers, one a believer and the other an atheist. When harvest came, the atheist taunted his believing neighbor. . . . His fields were rich with harvest, and he was sure to make a lot of money. "I thought you said it paid to believe in God and be a Christian," said the atheist. "It does pay," replied the Christian. "But God doesn't always pay his people in September."
—Warren Wiersbe
(Be Ready, 136)

It is God's grace that qualifies a person for millennial service and heaven, not suffering. But suffering, if properly responded to, exposes the quality of the person whom God's grace is transforming.
—Thomas Constable
(Notes on 2 Thessalonians, 9)

Blessed are you when people insult you, persecute you and falsely say all kinds of evil against you because of me. Rejoice and be glad, because great is your reward in heaven.
—Matthew 5:11–12

DIGGING DEEPER

The word "punish" in 1:8 is a strong word, and some use it to paint God as vindictive and angry, desiring to enact personal revenge on those who reject Jesus. However, this is not true. God is not angry with the sinner; he is angry with the sin. Have you ever heard someone use this argument against God? How could you counter this view by explaining more about the character of God?

7. Who is responsible to ensure that anyone who truly desires to know God will have that opportunity (2 Chronicles 16:9)?

8. God has given all people the choice to believe or reject him. Nevertheless, when we hear about the destiny of nonbelievers, we grieve. Can you suggest ways to interact with nonbelievers that you've found have softened their hearts toward the gospel?

9. Paul explains when God's ultimate righteous justice will occur in 1:7. This will happen when the Lord Jesus is revealed from heaven in blazing fire with his powerful angels. How is this event different from the rapture in 1 Thessalonians 4:16–17?

It's easy to become confused between the rapture and Jesus's return to earth after the tribulation to set up his millennial kingdom. The purpose of his first coming over two thousand years ago was to teach truth and provide the once-for-all sacrifice for our sins. I like to think of his second coming in two phases:

> In the first phase of the second coming, the rapture, Jesus snatches believers away to heaven to escape the earth's upcoming tribulation.
> In the second phase of the second coming, Jesus returns to earth, with raptured and resurrected believers, as judge to set up his millennial kingdom.

Paul wrote about the first phase of Jesus's second coming in his first letter and the second phase in his second letter. Just like in a thousand-piece puzzle, we must examine every nuance of all the pieces related to the end times passages to make sure we put them in the correct place.

10. Read Revelation 19:11–21, where the apostle John describes the second phase of the second coming in detail.

   List the words and names of the rider on the white horse. Who is this rider?

   Who accompanies the rider besides his powerful angels (Revelation 19:14; 3:5; 7:9)?

   What is his purpose (Revelation 19:11, 15)?

11. What does Zechariah 14:3–4, 9 reveal about this event?

Many scholars call this portion of the book of Revelation the battle of Armageddon. What can you learn about this battle, including its purpose?

If you're a believer, this will be your moment to shine—with the King! This is the glory that will make all suffering pale by comparison (Rom. 8:18). This will not be the closing curtain ending your life's drama, but the curtain unveiling a whole new stage, beginning a whole new play—one in which persecution and affliction have no part.
—Charles Swindoll
(*Steadfast Christianity*, 13)

Paul taught elsewhere that God will reward Christians, who endure the temptation to abandon their commitment to Jesus Christ, with the privilege of reigning with Christ in His millennial kingdom (2 Tim. 2:12). Whereas all Christians will enter the millennial kingdom at His Second Coming, only those who follow Him faithfully in this life will *reign with Him*.
—Thomas Constable
(*Notes on 2 Thessalonians*, 9)

12. Daniel also prophesied about this event (Daniel 7:13–14). What additional insight can you glean from this passage?

Paul encourages the Thessalonians with the inspiring hope that they will one day bask in God's glory in the millennial kingdom of God (2 Thessalonians 1:5, 10).

13. The Bible is full of "pictures" of the millennial kingdom. Choose several from the list below and share what you learn.

Micah 4:1–3

Isaiah 9:1–7

Isaiah 11:6–9

Isaiah 25:6–9

Isaiah 35

Revelation 20:1–6

Each of the three chapters of 2 Thessalonians ends with a prayer. Paul concludes this first part with a prayer for power.

14. Paul, Silas, Timothy, and probably other believers in Corinth, where Paul is writing from, join together regularly to pray for their brothers and sisters in Thessalonica (1:11–12). Why do the Thessalonians especially need power right then?

What kind of power do they ask for?

Why do you think Paul didn't ask God to remove the Thessalonians' suffering?

15. Do you need prayer for God's power in your life too? If so, share this need with your group or a friend.

16. Why do you think Paul often models Christians praying for one another in his writings? Why is prayer so instrumental to a committed Christian life?

near

by Misty Hedrick

o Lord, you walk a road that's near
but how, i sure can't tell
i only know that you are here
not out, through that rent veil

i draw you in like last of breath
your life awakens mine
you say you pull me back from death
invite me in to dine

i want to see your face, to know
but you hide out of sight
i'd peek, pass out, to meet that glow
of your so-brilliant light

the pain you witness in my eyes
lost darkness you find there
confusion, chaos, depth implies
the turmoil of my stare

you stand close, watch sun's pink glow
my daylight turns to twi'
o, guard my mind, so swift to slow
as la lune climbs the sky

i cannot carry on this way
without a hand to clutch
and though you're here, you always say
still i crave human touch

you're silent in the cool of day
you don't reach out, but why?
i'm tempted—can't you walk my way,
and let this cup pass by?

When Lawlessness Reigns

OPTIONAL

Memorize 1 Corinthians 14:40
But everything should be done in a fitting and orderly way.

On June 7, 1961, Yihiel Dinur broke down on the stand while testifying in the trial of Adolf Eichmann, mastermind of the Jewish Holocaust.

> In his brief statement, he [Dinur] suggested that Auschwitz was akin to a different world, a "planet of ashes," whose residents "had no names. . . . They didn't live according to the laws of the world here. . . . Their name was a number." (Green, "This Day in Jewish History")

However, years later in an interview with Mike Wallace for *60 Minutes*, Dinur admitted he no longer believed that Auschwitz was like living on a different planet. And he admitted his nervous collapse on the stand was due to a horrifying realization.

At that moment, Dinur said, "I was afraid about myself. I saw that I am capable to do this exactly like he." He realized that "Eichmann is in all of us."

Mike Wallace then addressed the camera, asking if Eichmann was a monster, a madman, "or something even more terrifying—was he normal?" (Thomas, "Musings on the Nature of Man and Evil Now News?").

Imagine a world where human depravity was given free rein. The Bible paints a picture of the last seven years of the current age—the tribulation—as a time of great lawlessness, lechery, and suffering. Paul learned that the Thessalonians feared that time was upon them and he wrote this second letter to calm their anxiety. In the process he added key pieces to the Scripture's end times puzzle for us.

 Read 2 Thessalonians 2:1–4.

1. What happened to confuse and unsettle the Thessalonians (2:1–2)?

As Henry Alford notes, "the coming of our Lord Jesus Christ" and "our gathering together to Him" both refer to the rapture of the church. Paul had used the term "the coming" (*parousia*) of the Lord four times in 1 Thessalonians (2:19; 3:13; 4:15; 5:23), and in every case it refers to the rapture. "Our gathering together to Him" also refers to what Paul wrote in 1 Thessalonians 4:17 about the rapture: "We . . . shall be caught up together with them [i.e., believers who have died in Christ] in the clouds to meet the Lord in the air" (*Greek Testament*, 3:288).

2. What is the difference between "the coming of our Lord Jesus Christ and our being gathered to him" in 2:1 and "the day of the Lord" in 2:2? Review the sidebar for clarity. Is this explanation helpful?

DIGGING DEEPER

In 2 Thessalonians 2:2, Paul encourages the Thessalonian church not to become "unsettled or alarmed" by the teaching that they are already in "the day of the Lord." The unique phrase in Greek, σαλευθῆναι ἀπὸ τοῦ νοό, is only found here. It refers to a shaking ship that has lost its way. Have you ever experienced losing your way regarding God's truths? How might Jesus's words in Luke 6:48 help you remain stable regardless of the shifting circumstances?

3. We don't know the motivation of the person who sent the fake letter supposedly from Paul, but why do you think some people commit these kinds of deceptions? How can we ensure that we don't become like them?

DIGGING DEEPER

The presence of the church is now delaying God's wrath on the earth. What happened in Genesis 19:12–29? In light of 2 Thessalonians and all that we have learned thus far, how was God's wrath held back in Sodom? What's holding it back now?

4. Paul assures the Thessalonians that despite the persecution they are experiencing, the day of the Lord has not commenced because two events that mark that day have not yet occurred. What are they (2:3)?

5. In Matthew 24:9–12, Jesus taught his disciples about the church's great apostasy during the tribulation. Paul called it "the rebellion." What did Jesus predict will happen during this widespread falling away?

6. What positive steps can you take to protect yourself and your church from departing from true doctrine?

7. According to 2 Thessalonians 2, in addition to pervasive apostasy, a "man of lawlessness" will rise up during the tribulation to lead the world. What do you learn about him from the following verses?

2 Thessalonians 2:3–4

1 John 2:18

DIGGING DEEPER

What more can you learn about the specifics of the "rebellion" from 2 Peter 3:3–7, Jude 17–19, and Revelation 17:1–5?

The word "rebellion" in Greek actually means *apostasy*—to depart from true doctrine, to fall away from the faith.

Paul was telling the Thessalonians, then, that this "day of the Lord" cannot come until there is a widespread departure from the true faith in God . . . on the part of the professing church. To a certain degree, apostasy is already here and is surging in strength and intensity . . . however, this present stage of turning away from the truth is just the beginning—just a faint foreshadow of the tsunami of error that is coming.
　　—John F. Walvoord and
　　　　Mark Hitchcock
(*1 & 2 Thessalonians*, 122–24)

At our worst, what are we capable of? If the worst selves of everyone on earth ever dominated, I suspect the whole world would resemble the Holocaust. What restrains our depravity now? Praise God, in this chapter Paul teaches us that God will never allow his own to experience a world like that!　—Sue

Throughout history there
have been many who have
done Satan's evil work (cf.
the "many antichrists,"
1 Jn. 2:18), and this is a
warning against over-hasty
identification of the man
of this chapter with any
historical personage. Paul's
concern is not with the evil
ones who appear from time
to time, but with the most
infamous of all, one who
will appear in the last days.
He never uses the term
"Antichrist," but plainly
he has in mind the being
John calls by this name.
—Leon Morris
(*1 and 2 Thessalonians*, 128)

Revelation 13:5–8

Daniel 8:23–25

8. What other event must also occur before the day of the Lord can begin (1 Thessalonians 4:16–17)? Why should this insight relieve their anxieties and soothe their fears? Why should it do the same for us?

 Read 2 Thessalonians 2:5–12.

9. In 2:5–6 Paul refers to a restraining power holding back "the man of lawlessness" until a predetermined time. Who do you think this restraining power is (Ephesians 1:13–14)?

10. Where does this restraining power reside right now (1 Corinthians 6:19; 3:16; John 14:15–18)? What difference do you think that makes in the world?

11. What are some of his ministries in our lives?

John 14:16–18; 16:13

John 14:26

John 15:26–27

John 16:8

John 16:12–15

Galatians 5:13–16, 26

Galatians 5:22–25

Lawlessness is presently working, but what keeps it from running wild is the Holy Spirit's ministry through Christian men and women. The Holy Spirit will not leave the earth when the Rapture occurs, since He is *always* omnipresent. But His ministry of restraining lawlessness through Christians in the church will cease, because the people whom He presently indwells will leave the earth.
—Thomas Constable
(*Notes on 2 Thessalonians*, 5)

12. In contrast, Paul paints a picture of our base nature without him (Galatians 5:19–21). Imagine and describe a world dominated by people like that.

When the Church is "gathered together" and taken to be with Christ in the air, the salt and light will be withdrawn. Then every vestige of goodness will decay; every remnant of truth, unravel. It is at that time when the man of lawlessness will take center stage. Like cages in a zoo suddenly opened, so will it be when the Restrainer is taken out of the way and lawlessness runs wild and rampant in the streets.
—Charles Swindoll
(*Steadfast Christianity*, 25)

13. In 2:7 Paul informs us that a time will come when the Holy Spirit will be "taken out of the way" so the Antichrist and his followers will have free rein to dominate the earth. How and when will that occur?

14. In 2:8, Paul describes the Antichrist's final defeat and demise. Who is the only one with the power to crush him? When will this occur? (Revelation 19:11, 16, 19–21)

15. Next, Paul reveals more about the time of the Antichrist's reign (2:9–10). How does he deceive the whole world so that people of every nation worship him as a god (Revelation 13:11–14)?

16. Where does rejection of God begin? Where does it end? (2:10–12; Psalm 50:16–21)

17. Why are those who reject God so vulnerable to deception?

18. In summary, why do the Thessalonians need to lay down their fears of the future and trust God? Why should Paul's comforting revelations quell their confusion and anxiety? What do you need in order to lay down your fears?

❋ Read 2 Thessalonians 2:13–17.

19. Why are Paul, Silas, and Timothy thanking God in 2:13? How are they different than those who reject the gospel (2:10)?

20. What do you think it means that believers will "share in the glory of our Lord Jesus Christ" (2:14)?

Revelation 20:6

Revelation 21:5–7

21. What precious resource has God provided for believers to help us live in this fallen world (2:15)? Do you take full advantage of this resource? Why or why not?

22. As usual, Paul ends this portion of his letter with a prayer (2:16–17). What words stand out to you in his prayer? What has God the Father and our Lord Jesus Christ given us, and how can this help us live well in an increasingly lawless world?

The Long-Sung Story

by Misty Hedrick

Did I miss it? Was he here?
He spoke of home on a different shore—the greener bank,
With its golden floor, and heaven like backlit sapphires.
But is it real? Did I miss him?
I heard no brass trumpet blast, not even a thunderclap,
No clouds opened just over my head to beam a gilded shaft
    down, and
No savior
Gracefully descended to lift my feet from this less-verdant hill.
Did I miss it? I don't want to stay here.
And that cold sleep beckoned, and I didn't want to fall asleep
    alone, abandoned.
Was it all fake news? Gullible, I drank it in like truth.
But wait.
Unrolled new scrolls let it fall—delicious
The words like honey dripped:
It hasn't happened
Yet.
I grayed. Time ran fast across my face
And still I cried out, my hands stretched as high as I could reach
The golden glint of glory paled in puffy chestnut eyes,
But the clouds stayed tightly gathered, like the old priest's robe
    tied with a scarlet cord.
Spinning planets rose and fell,
But no savior beckoned.
Deliver me. Please don't forget me.
I reached higher, strained to the shelf with the scrolls
    turned yellow
Frayed at the edges, worn thin as years chafed my skin
The honeyed words now etched deep in the forefront of
    my mind
Still I opened the seal and let it unravel . . .
I know. I know. I know. But I don't want to be here. Come now.
Hold on—was that a crack in the veiled ether?
Danger swarms encircled me, and oh, yes
Still stung.
My skin cried out, swelling fiercely.
How long? When will you step down and rescue me?
    Don't leave me here.

Where hate dammed the mercy river
Fear split skin colors, justice falls faint
And frigid love twists, runs, and hides for lack of faith.
And the other, greener shore seems farther out of sight, mist
    shrouded
And my polished hope wears as fragile as the ancient
    rolled-up pages.
More than mere anecdote—Christ, the long-sought antidote.
One sweetened omega—that's all I asked—
When frozen slumber breaks and
The stingers that chased me finally fall smashed
And the stony-sleep lullaby gives way to the sound of
    gravestones rolling
And bodies meet souls ascending like he did
In that long-sung, crinkled, rising-up story—
Oh, I tell his people *that*.
Good news. True news. He's-coming-for-you news.
But it hasn't happened
Yet.

Whistle While You Wait

Here's a true handed-down family story: While my husband's great-grandmother was shelling peas, a sliver of something stuck deep under her fingernail. Preoccupied with other chores, she failed to tend to it even though it grew sore, red, and festered. In time the infection spread through her whole body; she became septic and died. Over time in the Body of Christ, sin can spread a toxic poison that results in chaos, disharmony, factions, and if never dealt with, the death of the church.

Because of doctrinal confusion, some in the infant Thessalonian church had adopted sinful life patterns that, if ignored, Paul knew would erupt in serious problems for the church later. These idlers determined that since Jesus would come for them soon, they no longer needed to work. Paul had warned this group twice in his first letter (1 Thessalonians 4:11–12 and 5:14), but they refused to repent and had become freeloaders and a burden to the church.

Resentment was building, as it always does in these situations, and Paul responds with a strong rebuke. Interwoven life lessons abound for us all in this final section of Paul's second letter to the Thessalonians.

Read 2 Thessalonians 3.

1. Paul hasn't shared much about his own struggles in Corinth, where, in addition to his tent-making profession, he's working diligently to plant another church. Paul begins with a prayer request (3:1–2). What does he ask for? In your opinion, why?

OPTIONAL

Memorize Galatians 6:9–10

Let us not become weary in doing good, for at the proper time we will reap a harvest if we do not give up. Therefore, as we have opportunity, let us do good to all people, especially to those who belong to the family of believers.

DIGGING DEEPER

The phrase "be honored" in 3:1 can also be translated "to be glorified." Take a look at Acts 13:48. What happens when the Word of God is glorified? How can you personally "glorify" the Scriptures?

In 3:3–5 Paul turns his thoughts back to the Thessalonians, expressing his love, confidence, and trust in them. Encouraging words of unconditional love often need to precede correction.

2. Instead of rebuking the disobedient believers again, Paul addresses the obedient believers. What does he tell them to do? How does he want them to think about and treat these idlers who were endangering the unity and stability of the church family?

3:6

3:14

3:15

3. What effect do you think Paul's words in 3:5, 14–15 might have on those refusing to heed Paul's instruction? What do you think Paul hopes?

4. What was your initial reaction to Paul's command in verse 6? Why?

5. Although healthy discipline isn't popular today and it's difficult to administer, why is it necessary both in the family and in the church family (Hebrews 12:11; Proverbs 5:23; 13:18)?

DIGGING DEEPER

For more in-depth study on divine discipline, dig into Hebrews 12:4–13 and 1 Corinthians 5:1–12. What do you learn about the church's responsibilities in response to extremely serious sin that has festered until it is polluting the whole Body of Christ?

6. What had Paul, Silas, and Timothy done while they were in Thessalonica to back up their instructions (3:7–10)? Why did they do this?

7. Did these evangelists and church planters have the right to ask for support from the Thessalonians while they ministered to them (1 Corinthians 9:13–14)? Why do you think they didn't demand that right in this situation?

Every Christian worker has the right to support from the church as he serves the Lord (Luke 10:7; Gal. 6:6; 1 Tim. 5:17–18). We must not use Paul's example as an excuse not to support God's servants. But any servant of God has the privilege of setting aside that right to the glory of God. Paul did this so that he might be an example to the young believers in Thessalonica.
—Warren Wiersbe
(*Be Ready*, 175)

8. What do Paul's actions and attitudes teach us about when it's good for us to demand our rights and when it isn't?

9. In 3:10 we hear the core reason Paul is delivering these confrontational words. What are some of the consequences of an "idle" lifestyle (3:11)? In your opinion, why are these the natural results of refusing to work? Why do idlers irritate and anger others?

10. Who ordained that mankind should work (Genesis 1:28–29)?

11. What was mankind's first job (Genesis 2:5, 15)? Do you think this job was pleasurable? Why or why not?

12. Who was man's first co-worker (Genesis 2:18–22)?

13. When did work become difficult (Genesis 3:17–19)? Why?

14. Even though work is more difficult today, in what ways is it still pleasurable? What do you think is the purpose of work?

15. What kinds of work have you enjoyed throughout your life? Share some of the benefits.

16. Do you think there will be work in the millennial kingdom and the new heaven and the new earth? Why or why not? If so, what kind of work would you like to do there?

17. What is a busybody (2 Thessalonians 3:11; 1 Timothy 5:13)? Why do you think idleness easily leads to being disruptive and a busybody? Have you observed these characteristics in a church? If so, what kinds of problems resulted?

Go to the ant, you sluggard; consider its ways and be wise!
—Proverbs 6:6

18. How does Paul counsel anyone who tends toward laziness (3:12)?

For in this hope we were saved. Now hope that is seen is not hope. For who hopes for what he sees? But if we hope for what we do not see, we wait for it with patience.
—Romans 8:24–25 (ESV)

19. What are his words of wisdom for us all (3:13)? Do you tend to be lazy when you know it's wise to be active and productive? What would taking his counsel to heart mean for you in your everyday life?

20. Once again Paul ends this section of his letter with a final prayer of blessing. What does Paul pray for the Thessalonians and for all believers (3:16, 18)? Why is this blessing particularly meaningful for the situation the Thessalonians and many of us face?

21. Think back through the study. How have Paul's two letters to the Thessalonians given you a sense of hope? What have you learned about your life now and in the future that encourages you to move forward with faith and endurance?

Seeking Shelter

by Misty Hedrick

I never heard the voice of God
Nor saw the Savior face to face
I never felt his gentle hand
His healing warmth, did not embrace.

I searched for peaceful prismed gems
On burnished beaches brazen lay
Ashamed from smelt-hard heart of stone
Burnt time all wasted, washed away.

I waked abroad and wandered far
I read and riffed through stacks of books
I begged for God to meet with me
On paths, in pubs, and comfy nooks.

Alone, unknown, and prone to wrong
I wondered why such fear infused
As tearful sleepless nights passed by
You spoke—but listen? I refused.

I choked, my splattered soul, sin-sick
"You're worthless," rhythmic voices churned.
I knelt, and for forgiveness begged:
I fell, I'm lost—when will I learn?

When late one day we meet at last
You say no condemnation here
Your child in Christ without constraint
Awaits a coronation cheer.

Acknowledgments

With special thanks to my two gifted and diligent Dallas Theological Seminary interns Misty Hedrick and Nandi Roszhart, for their excellent contributions on this project.

Handy Glossary of End Times Terms

1. Heaven: The Bible informs us that if we are "in Christ," when we die we will not cease to exist. At that moment, our physical body and our spirit separate. Our physical body stays on earth, but our spirit immediately goes to heaven. Until the rapture, our spirit is in the conscious presence of the Lord in heaven, or paradise. "For we know that if the earthly tent we live in is destroyed, we have a building from God, an eternal house in heaven, not built by human hands. Meanwhile we groan, longing to be clothed instead with our heavenly dwelling" (2 Corinthians 5:1–2).

When Jesus was on the cross, the repentant criminal on the adjacent cross cried out, "Jesus, remember me when you come into your kingdom." Jesus answered him, "Truly I tell you, today you will be with me in paradise" (Luke 23:42–43). Notice Jesus used the term "paradise" rather than "kingdom" since he won't usher in his millennial kingdom on the earth until the end of the tribulation.

What is heaven, and where is it? It's always referred to as "up," so we can assume it's an atmospheric place beyond our physical reach. Our conscious spirits dwell there with the Lord as we wait for the consummation of history as we know it. The rapture will begin that consummation.

2. The rapture: The word means "caught up, snatched suddenly." Renowned end times scholar Mark Hitchcock defines it this way: "Simply stated, the Rapture of the church, which is the first phase of Christ's [second] coming, is the intersection of two events: the resurrection of the dead, specifically only believers, and the transformation of living believers. They will all be immediately together in Jesus' glorious presence, and He will escort them to heaven" (*The End*, 125).

Two passages provide details: 1 Thessalonians 4:13–5:11 and 1 Corinthians 15:42–58.

> According to the Lord's word, we tell you that we who are still alive, who are left until the coming of the Lord, will certainly not precede those who have fallen asleep. For the Lord himself will

come down from heaven, with a loud command, with the voice of the archangel and with the trumpet call of God, and the dead in Christ will rise first. After that, we who are still alive and are left will be caught up together with them in the clouds to meet the Lord in the air. And so we will be with the Lord forever. (1 Thessalonians 4:15–17)

At that time, those of us who have died physically will experience the uniting of our physical body with our disembodied spirit that has been waiting in heaven for this day. Paul informs us that on the day of the rapture, we will receive our new resurrected bodies. Read 1 Corinthians 15:42–58 for the incredibly exciting details. A number of biblical passages suggest that the rapture occurs before the tribulation. According to many scholars, the rapture could occur at any time.

3. *"The coming wrath" in 1 Thessalonians 5:9:* "For God did not appoint us to suffer wrath but to receive salvation through our Lord Jesus Christ."

Scripture is clear—God's judgment is coming. Will any of us escape? Yes, on the cross, Jesus delivered all who receive him as their Savior from "the coming wrath." But when will it come? In this passage, is Paul referring to God's eternal wrath that, sadly, unbelievers will experience at the great white throne judgment (Revelation 20:11–15)? Possibly. But it seems much more likely that here in 1 Thessalonians 5:9 he's talking to Christians about a particular time of wrath on the earth that is still future.

In addition, Paul praises the Thessalonians in 1 Thessalonians 1:10 because they are waiting for Jesus, who will, in some way, rescue them from this coming wrath, and later (4:13–18) he informs them about a time when Jesus will snatch them up and away from the earth, the place where this horrific wrath will soon unfold. The book of Revelation describes this wrath in detail in chapters 5–19. Theologians have labeled these horrendous seven years on earth "the tribulation."

Where are Christians during this time? We are above it all, in heaven with the Lord, clearly seen in passages like Revelation 4, 5, 7:9–17, and 19:1–10. How like our loving God to call us away from the chaos, destruction, and turmoil, secure with him and our brothers and sisters from every place and century. How natural that we would praise God together, singing, "You are worthy, our Lord and God, to receive glory and honor and power" (Revelation 4:11). Is it any wonder Paul writes in 1 Thessalonians 4:18, "Therefore encourage one another with these words"?

4. *The tribulation:* Jesus spoke of a time on the earth of unprecedented destruction and chaos. When his disciples asked him, "When will this happen, and what will be the sign of your coming and of the end of the age?" (Matthew 24:3), he told them, "For then there will be great distress,

unequaled from the beginning of the world until now—and never to be equaled again" (verse 21).

Many scholars have synchronized all the Bible texts that relate to this terrible time and have determined this will take place after believers are raptured to heaven, where they will experience the judgment seat of Christ for rewards, as well as other glorious events, while the tribulation takes place on the earth. Working with various biblical timetables, they believe the tribulation will last for seven years and will end when Jesus and the raptured believers return to earth to bring justice and inaugurate Jesus's millennial kingdom (Revelation 19:11–20:6).

5. The kingdom: This word has several nuanced meanings. In one sense, when Jesus came to earth the first time, he brought aspects of the kingdom with him. We know about God's righteousness and holiness that characterize the kingdom.

But the Bible also reveals another kingdom—a glorious future kingdom that Christ will inaugurate on the earth after the tribulation. While we are in heaven during this time of intense turmoil on the earth, Revelation 5:9–10 records a song we will sing to Jesus: "You are worthy to take the scroll and to open its seals, because you were slain, and with your blood you purchased for God persons from every tribe and language and people and nation. You have made them to be a kingdom and priests to serve our God, and they will reign on the earth."

We won't be floating on clouds, playing harps for eternity. This passage reveals that believers will rule and reign, serve and lead with Christ in that glorious millennial kingdom for a thousand years. That's why in 1 Thessalonians 2:12, Paul urges all Christians "to live lives worthy of God, who calls you into his kingdom and glory."

I suspect that our roles and what we do there will be determined by who we are and what we do here. We will find out what that entails right after we are raptured and appear in heaven before the bema, the judgment seat of Christ.

6. The judgment seat of Christ (aka the bema seat): Jesus often told us to expect rewards for what we do on earth. For example, "But love your enemies, do good to them, and lend to them without expecting to get anything back. Then your reward will be great" (Luke 6:35).

In his second letter to the Corinthians, Paul explains that when we die physically, our spirit separates from our body for a time while we wait for Jesus to resurrect our bodies during the rapture. He goes on to tell us about another important event in our eternal lives—the time we stand before Jesus to give an account of our earthly lives, receive any rewards we have earned, and learn about what we will be and do when we reign with Christ and serve as priests in his millennial kingdom (Revelation 4:9–10).

This moment, called the judgment seat of Christ, or the bema seat, happens right after the rapture.

> Therefore we are always confident and know that as long as we are at home in the body we are away from the Lord. For we live by faith, not by sight. We are confident, I say, and would prefer to be away from the body and at home with the Lord. So we make it our goal to please him, whether we are at home in the body or away from it. For we must all appear before the judgment seat of Christ, so that each of us may receive what is due us for the things done while in the body, whether good or bad. (2 Corinthians 5:6–10)

First, let's be clear. The judgment seat does not determine whether or not you are saved from the wrath of God. If you have accepted Jesus as your Savior, you will never experience the great white throne judgment, where nonbelievers will be judged. This bema judgment is not to punish sin, but believers are still accountable to God, as Paul states in 1 Corinthians 4:2–5:

> Now it is required that those who have been given a trust must prove faithful. I care very little if I am judged by you or by any human court; indeed, I do not even judge myself. My conscience is clear, but that does not make me innocent. It is the Lord who judges me. Therefore judge nothing before the appointed time; wait until the Lord comes. He will bring to light what is hidden in darkness and will expose the motives of the heart. At that time each will receive their *praise* from God. (emphasis added)

The Greek word for "judgment seat," *bema*, refers to a raised platform like where the judge sits in a courtroom, or where rewards are distributed at athletic games.

What's the purpose of the bema? To assess the quality of our service. I must admit I find this truth frightening. I know my motives aren't always pure, and I don't want to serve Jesus to gain notoriety or to feel good about myself, but sometimes I do. However, I hope this realization sobers my intentions and causes me to lay aside those ugly ulterior motives. And then I simply must rely on his mercy and grace. In some just way, Jesus will assess the value of what we've become and done and reward us accordingly. What kinds of service does he value? A look at different kinds of "crowns" may provide some insight.

7. *Crowns:* Jesus advised Christians to do good works to please God and not other people: "Be careful not to practice your righteousness in front of others to be seen by them. If you do, you will have no reward from your Father in heaven" (Matthew 6:1). The Bible also mentions specific honors called "crowns" that will be given for specific practices:

The crown of rejoicing (1 Thessalonians 2:19) for believers who lead others to Christ

The crown of glory (1 Peter 5:1–4) for shepherding God's people graciously and faithfully

The crown of righteousness (2 Timothy 4:8) for believers who long for Jesus's return and live a righteous life in light of that reality

The crown of life (James 1:12; Revelation 2:10) for believers who endure suffering for their faith, even unto death

The imperishable crown (1 Corinthians 9:24–25) for believers who exhibit consistent self-discipline leading to victory

What will we do with these crowns? We will fall down at the feet of Jesus and lay our crowns before him in humble recognition of the reality that he enabled us to achieve these honors. These awards may also influence what we do in the coming millennial kingdom (Luke 19:11–26).

Works Cited

Alford, Henry. *The Greek Testament*. 4 vols. Cambridge: Deighton, Bell, and Co., 1883, 1881, 1880, 1884.

Chandler, Matt. *The Explicit Gospel*. Wheaton, IL: Crossway, 2012. Kindle.

Constable, Thomas L. *Notes on Acts*. Sonic Light. 2021 edition. https://planobiblechapel.org/tcon/notes/pdf/acts.pdf.

———. *Notes on 1 Thessalonians*. Sonic Light. 2021 edition. https://planobiblechapel.org/tcon/notes/pdf/1thessalonians.pdf.

———. *Notes on 2 Thessalonians*. Sonic Light. 2021 edition. https://planobiblechapel.org/tcon/notes/pdf/2thessalonians.pdf.

Edgar, Thomas R. "An Exegesis of Rapture Passages." In *Issues in Dispensationalism*, edited by Wesley R. Willis and John R. Master, 206–7. Chicago: Moody Press, 1994.

Edwards, Jada. IF:Lead. Dallas, September 26, 2019. https://www.ifgathering.com/iflead2019/.

Edwards, Sue, Kelley Mathews, and Henry J. Rogers. *Mixed Ministry: Working Together as Brothers and Sisters in an Oversexed Society*. Grand Rapids: Kregel Academic and Professional, 2008.

Ferguson, Everett. *Backgrounds of Early Christianity*. 3rd ed. Grand Rapids: Eerdmans, 2003.

Graham, Billy. "Making a Difference in an Age of Crisis: Why There Is Still Hope, and How You Can Be Part of What God Is Doing." *Decision Magazine*, July 2014. https://decisionmagazine.com/making-a-difference-in-an-age-of-crisis/.

Green, David B. "This Day in Jewish History: Novelist Who Taught Israelis About the Holocaust." Haaretz.com, May 15, 2014. https://www.haaretz.com/jewish/.premium-novelist-who-taught-israelis-about-the-holocaust-1.5248468.

Hellerman, Joseph H. *When the Church Was a Family: Recapturing Jesus' Vision for Authentic Christian Community*. Nashville: B & H Academic, 2009.

Hendricks, Howard G., and William D. Hendricks. *Living by the Book: The Art and Science of Reading the Bible*. Chicago: Moody Press, 2007.

Hitchcock, Mark. *The End: A Complete Overview of Bible Prophecy and the End of Days*. Carol Stream, IL: Tyndale, 2012.

Hogg, C. F., and W. E. Vine. *The Epistles of Paul the Apostle to the Thessalonians*. Glasgow: Pickering & Inglis, n.d.

Holmes, Michael W. *1 & 2 Thessalonians*. NIV Application Commentary. Grand Rapids: Zondervan, 1998.

Jackman, David. *The Authentic Church: A Study of the Letters to the Thessalonians*. Fearn, Ross-shire, Scotland: Christian Focus, 1998.

Jeffers, Susan. *Feel the Fear . . . and Do It Anyway*. New York: Ballantine, 1987.

Landsberg, Mitchell. "Preacher's Rapture Forecasts Fizzled." *Los Angeles Times*, December 18, 2013. https://www.latimes.com/local/obituaries/la-xpm-2013-dec-18-la-me-harold-camping-20131218-story.html.

Lewis, C. S. *Mere Christianity: Combining The Case for Christianity, Christian Behaviour, Beyond Personality*. New York: Macmillan, 1960.

———. *The Problem of Pain: How Human Suffering Raises Almost Intolerable Intellectual Problems*. New York: Macmillan, 1962.

Maraboli, Steve. *Unapologetically You: Reflections on Life and the Human Experience*. Port Washington, NY: A Better Today Publishing, 2013. Kindle.

Morris, Leon. *1 and 2 Thessalonians*. Tyndale New Testament Commentaries. Downers Grove, IL: IVP Academic, 1984.

Murray, John. *The Epistle to the Romans*. 2 vols. New International Commentary on the New Testament. Grand Rapids: Eerdmans, 1959.

Newbell, Trillia. "Meet the Family of God." DesiringGod.org, February 27, 2014. https://www.desiringgod.org/articles/meet-the-family-of-god.

Osborne, Grant R. *1 & 2 Thessalonians: Verse by Verse*, edited by Elliott Ritzema and Danielle Thevenaz. Osborne New Testament Commentaries. Bellingham, WA: Lexham, 2018.

Ryrie, Charles. "First and Second Thessalonians." *Ryrie Study Bible*. Chicago: Moody Publishers, 1985.

Shirer, Priscilla. *The Armor of God*. Nashville: LifeWay, 2015.

Smith, James K. A. *Desiring the Kingdom*. Grand Rapids: Baker Academic, 2009. Kindle.

Stott, John R. W. *The Message of 1 and 2 Thessalonians: The Bible Speaks Today*. Downers Grove, IL: IVP Academic, 1991.

Swindoll, Charles R. *Steadfast Christianity: A Study of Second Thessalonians*. Fullerton, CA: Insight for Living, 1986.

———. *1 & 2 Thessalonians*. Swindoll's Living Insights New Testament Commentary. Carol Stream, IL: Tyndale, 2016.

Tarn, W. W., and G. T. Griffith. *Hellenistic Civilisation*. 3rd ed. London: E. Arnold, 1952.

Thomas, Cal. "Musings on the Nature of Man and Evil Now News?" *Sun Sentinel*, April 5, 1996. https://www.sun-sentinel.com/news/fl-xpm-1996-04-05-9604080104-story.html.

Turner, Laura. "Why Are So Many Christians Obsessed with Predicting the Rapture?" *Pacific Standard*, April 19, 2019. https://psmag.com

/news/why-are-so-many-christians-obsessed-with-predicting-the
-rapture.

Voskamp, Ann. *The Broken Way: A Daring Path into the Abundant Life.*
Grand Rapids: Zondervan, 2016. Kindle.

Walvoord, John F. *The Thessalonian Epistles.* Bible Study Commentary.
Grand Rapids: Zondervan, 1979.

Walvoord, John F., and Mark Hitchcock. *1 & 2 Thessalonians.* John Walvoord Prophecy Commentaries, edited by Philip E. Rawley. Chicago:
Moody Publishers, 2012.

Weima, Jeffrey A. D. *1–2 Thessalonians.* Baker Exegetical Commentary of
the New Testament. Grand Rapids: Baker Academic, 2014.

Wiersbe, Warren. *Be Ready: Living in Light of Christ's Return.* Colorado
Springs: David C. Cook, 1979.

———. *The Bible Exposition Commentary.* Vol. 2. Wheaton, IL: Victor
Books, 1996.

Willard, Dallas. *The Divine Conspiracy.* HarperCollins e-Books, 2014.
http://rbdigital.oneclickdigital.com.

Wright, N. T. *Surprised by Hope: Rethinking Heaven, the Resurrection, and the
Mission of the Church.* New York: HarperOne, 2014.

FOR FURTHER READING

Dillow, Joseph C. *The Reign of the Servant Kings: A Study of Eternal Secu-
rity and the Final Significance of Man.* Hayesville, NC: Schoettle, 1992,
574–81.

Hitchcock, Mark. *The End: A Complete Overview of Bible Prophecy and the
End of Days.* Carol Stream, IL: Tyndale, 2012, 211–12.

About the Author

Sue Edwards is professor of educational ministries and leadership (her specialization is women's studies) at Dallas Theological Seminary, where she has equipped men and women for future ministry for over twenty years. Before teaching in the academy, she ministered as a Bible teacher, curriculum writer, and overseer of several megachurch women's ministries. As minister to women at Irving Bible Church and director of women's ministry at Prestonwood Baptist Church in Dallas, she has worked with women of all walks of life, ages, and stages. Her passion is to see modern and postmodern women connect, learn from one another, and bond around God's Word. Her Bible studies have ushered thousands of women all over the country and overseas into deeper Scripture study and community experiences.

With Kelley Mathews, Sue has coauthored *Organic Ministry to Women: A Guide to Transformational Ministry with Next Generation Women*; *Women's Retreats: A Creative Planning Guide*; and *Leading Women Who Wound: Strategies for an Effective Ministry*. Sue and Kelley joined with Henry Rogers to coauthor *Mixed Ministry: Working Together as Brothers and Sisters in an Oversexed Society*. *Organic Mentoring: A Mentor's Guide to Relationships with Next Generation Women*, coauthored with Barbara Neumann, explores the new values, preferences, and problems of the next generation and shows mentors how to avoid potential land mines and how to mentor successfully. Her newest book, *Invitation to Educational Ministry: Foundations of Transformative Christian Education*, coedited with George M. Hillman Jr., DTS vice president of education and professor of educational ministries and leadership, serves as a primary academic textbook for schools all over the country, as well as a handbook for church leaders.

Sue has a doctor of ministry degree from Gordon-Conwell Theological Seminary in Boston, a master's in Bible from Dallas Theological Seminary, and a bachelor's degree in journalism from Trinity University. With Dr. Joye Baker, she oversees the DTS doctor of educational ministries degree program, with a women-in-ministry emphasis.

Sue has been married to David forty-nine years. They have two married daughters, Heather and Rachel, and five grandchildren. David is a retired CAD applications engineer and a lay prison chaplain. Sue loves fine chocolates and exotic coffees, romping with her grandchildren, and taking walks with David and her two West Highland terriers, Quigley and Emma Jane.

Notes

Notes

Notes

Notes

Notes

Notes